SONGS FROM UNDER THE EL

THE EL

Memories of Life in the Dark

Joanne de Simone

Moonlight Garden
Publications
Renton, Washington

www.stramal.com
www.joannedesimone-writer.com

ISBNs: 978-1-938281-52-5 (paperback)
        978-1-938281-23-5 (large print paperback)
        978-1-938281-51-8 (e-book)

Library of Congress Control Number: 2021920273

Published 2021, Moonlight Garden Publications, an imprint of Gazebo Gardens Publishing, LLC, Renton, WA
www.GazeboGardensPublishing.com

Printed in the United States of America.

For my mother, Frances,
stronger than the steel El
we were raised under.

Special thanks to my friend,
Roger Chillemi,
for lovingly restoring
my treasured family photographs
and creating the cover art design.

TABLE OF CONTENTS

PROLOGUE
MY STORY

Why not call it a memoir? Memoirs are what famous people write. I am not famous; however, I have always desired what my late friend Mal called "anonymous fame." It's the kind of recognition where people know of you, and enjoy your work, but do not recognize you in public. It allows for quiet success without the entourage.

This book is about memories—mostly mine. Other stories were told to me by my mother and father and a couple of aunts and uncles. Some of the memories can be described as perceptions. Perhaps some have been embellished, or even partly fabricated; I don't remember.

Memories are personal, certainly subjective. They cannot be summoned chronologically, for that would impair the journey and their beauty. Let's save that for the history books. Memories come to us through our senses, like flashes and snippets of déjà vu. They take us away for a very brief time, only to vanish—and in a wink, we are back in the present. I wanted to hold on to these memories long enough to write them down, before "...as a flower of the field...the wind passes over it, and it is gone, and its place remembers it no more." (Psalm 103:15).

Should these memories differ from those of the De Simones or my other relatives, they should write their own book. (When I became a writer, I decided to use de Simone...I thought it looked chic. But, no matter how we spell it, I am a De Simone.)

This book is dedicated to my mother, Frances. Its thread belongs to my Father, Joseph (Giuseppe). But, the memories are written for my nieces and nephews: Francine, Richard, Darren, Eric, Catherine, Cheryl, Christina, Joseph, and my "adopted" niece, Roseann, and for their children. It is my desire that all of them, and those who come after them, will embrace the ridiculous, tiny bit scandalous, sometimes tragic, hopefully humorous story of those who came before.

It was with pride and determination that I put my heart into writing this book. I don't want the kids to think that they were just hatched somewhere in the desert! More importantly, my hope is that they keep telling the story...and keep telling the story...and keep telling...

– J. de Simone

CHAPTER ONE
BEGINNINGS

In the beginning...not that it's biblical or epic, but I should start at the beginning, when my memories began, and when I began remembering the family stories that were told to me. I come from a family of immigrants. My father's side is from Calabria. My mother's parents came from Naples and Abruzzo. My grandparents' first stop in America was—as was for all immigrants from that time—at Ellis Island, where a vowel or 2 might have been dropped from family names, or in some cases, outright anglicized by an Irish clerk.

The title of this book refers to where I grew up, and how I grew up, under the "El," or elevated train. This was a term that was added to my grandparents' limited English word stock and not known to any of my Italian ancestors before they moved to Brooklyn.

The El is not just a description of how a train travels, i.e., the subway is underground. The El is the steel frame that runs parallel to buildings and holds the train high above the ground. In my time, it was also used to describe your living conditions—your social status. Either you lived under the El, and people thought you were poor, or you lived *around the corner* with the somewhat middle class where it had no bearing on your life whatsoever.

My maternal grandfather, Antonio Ferro, was born in Abruzzo, Italy, on or about February 28, 1874. He was about 6' 2" tall with reddish blonde wavy hair, striking blue eyes, and a very becoming mustache. Antonio left Italy in 1895 to travel around South America. His reason for sailing was, as rumor had it, to find some new oats to sow, since he had deflowered every willing maiden in Abruzzo and all its neighboring villages.

In addition to making love to all the women he could get his hands on, he made his living with his hands, making shoes. Not repairing shoes, but making shoes—Italian shoes, the kind women love to own. He went back to Italy for a short time in 1902 then sailed to America from Bovalino. At the age of 27, on April 5, 1902, he arrived in Manhattan to check out the oats on the gold-paved American streets of New York City. On May 28, 1903, he visited some friends (or perhaps, distant cousins?) on Mulberry Street in Manhattan's Little Italy.

In the small tenement apartment, seated at the kitchen table, was a somber looking woman with long, black hair knotted severely in a bun. She had arrived in New York the previous day on a ship that sailed from Naples, Italy. Her tallness (5' 7") was lost in her wideness, so that she appeared to be very round with a cupcake on her head. Even the loveliness of her dark eyes and full, red lips were eclipsed by a triple chin that seemed to begin at her ears and descend to her huge bosom.

Antonio immediately inquired with his friend, Giovanni. "Who is she? Is she married? Can I take her out on the town?"

Giovanni stopped him short and explained a few things about the woman at the table. "Her name is Emelia Cardella. She's my wife's cousin. Her family sent her here from the old country to get married. She's 26—an old maid, you know. We arranged a marriage for her here with a plumber from Bari. He lives down the block. He took a look at her and said he wasn't interested. Too fat. What can we do now? Send her back to Italy in shame and disgrace? She's staying with us until we can figure out what to do with her."

At this, Antonio repeated his request to take her out on the town. Giovanni shook his head and made it clear that Emelia was a good girl, and if Antonio wanted to take her to town, he'd have to marry her first. So, about 3 weeks later, Emelia Cardella, born on June 2, 1877, in a little town outside Naples, Italy (which has been pronounced as Sessana, but not easy to find on the map), married Antonio Ferro. Their wedding took place on June 18, 1903, in a civil ceremony at New York's City Hall. I don't know why they weren't married in church, as Grandma was very religious.

My grandfather figured that since she held on to her virginity for 26 years, she must be guarding something special. There, he was mistaken. She was special in her own way, but the flower she was protecting turned out to be garden variety, as it usually is.

It didn't matter. They had a typical marriage for the times, and he remained fairly faithful to her. Emelia bore 10 children, 6 of which grew to adulthood—Giovanni, Filomena, Luisa, Francesca, Silvestri, and Americo. When they went to school, they came home being called John, Phyllis, Louise, Frances, Caesar, and Rico. Their family lived on 78th Street, off the El, in the lovely ground-floor apartment of a 2-family house that Antonio owned.

Seems Grandpa gave up the shoes and opened a trash carting business, which went bust during the Great Depression. My mother said he was never the same again, that he felt like a failure. He lost the house, but his cousin, who owned the house across the street, gave the family the 1st-floor apartment. It was like a mansion.

That's the place where all the aunts, uncles, and cousins had wonderful times—up until I was about 3 years old. (It's also the place where my brother Richard got his hand caught in the washing machine wringer. Luckily, Frances turned off the machine before Richard became a permanent "righty.") Antonio Ferro died in February 1947, a few days before his 73rd birthday, from what was described as natural causes and senility—now known by a harder word to spell—Alzheimer's disease. I never knew him.

At Grandma's, the birthday parties were wonderful. The dining table was set, fit for royalty. Linen and lace tablecloths. Delicate china and crystal. Birthday cakes in tiers. Aunt Louise used to cut the cakes by wetting a glass, sticking it in the center of the cake, and taking it out to leave a hole so the slices were cut evenly. At these treasured events, soda (or "pop" as it's called west of the Hudson) was served. Hoffman black cherry, cream, and other flavors. Not anyone's birthday? No soda. Just milk and water, and always lots of strong coffee.

My mother took hundreds of pictures over the years, kept them in a shoebox. When relatives visited, they helped themselves. There are still many photographs, somewhere, that describe the happy life. I even have a few remnants from my mother's National Shoes box. When I shied away from any and all photos of me, she always told me that I would be sorry someday. She was right. I look at those pictures, in their black-and-white glory, and search for something that I didn't see before.

In 1952, when my brother Joseph was born, Grandma Emelia was dropped off at our hole of an apartment at 8018 New Utrecht Avenue. Her sisters told my mother that she had to "take care of Mama," and my mother not only obeyed, but also considered it an honor. As a dutiful wife (to a philandering husband), she asked his permission.

My mother, until the day she died, told me that my father was enthusiastic about it, saying, "Of course, Frances, that's your mother." (What did he care? He was gone half the time, anyway.)

It was Grandma that did most of the food preparation and gave Frances instructions, as Grandma could not stand on her feet at all, let alone stir the sauce (which we called gravy) every 5 minutes. Coming from Naples, she was big on fish, all kinds. We even had eels swimming in the bathtub on Christmas Eve, which eventually were hacked and served up. (Kill me.)

Grandma lived with us until she died of a massive heart attack on July 4, 1957. I would imagine that her heart couldn't keep up with the 300 pounds in its care. She had gone to a nursing home for a short stay, after a minor surgery, and when my mother and Uncle Rico went to pick her up, the doctor gave them the bad news. Frances was convinced that the nurse dropped Grandma, and that the fall brought on the attack. I don't know.

Grandma Emelia was to have 2 granddaughters named for her. One died when she was 3 days old, and the other at 9 months. Superstition got the better of the family, and Grandma Emelia took the name with her to the grave.

THE SILENT SIDE

All that is known about the beginnings of Domenico De Simone, my paternal grandfather, (which has been told to me by relatives) is that he came to America on March 9, 1896, at the age of 22. He met and married

Francesca Frotta, a 20-year-old girl who came from the same village in Calabria. Francesca was, in contrast to Emelia, a very small woman, not 5' tall. She had a tiny waist, oversized breasts, and huge, black eyes—bedroom eyes, as they were called in those days. More about her later.

The other significant—or perhaps, sentimental—whens, whys, and hows are still a mystery and will remain so. The anyones and everyones who knew anything are dead, and if a De Simone that's still with us knows more, they are not talking. The De Simones don't talk. We do know that the De Simone ancestors migrated from France at some point way, way back, or so we were told. As I said, nobody ever talked about anything in my father's family. And, it still remains a tight-lipped clan.

Domenico and Francesca married in Brooklyn, New York in 1899 (?) and started a farm. Yes, a real farm in Brooklyn with cows, chickens, and everything that went with it. They had 6 children—4 boys and 2 girls: Giovanni, Giuseppe, Antonio, Italia, Arturo, and Annella.

One of the boys was my father, Giuseppe, known as Gi (pronounced Gee) to the family. He was the only one of the children to actually work the farm, or so I was told by Aunt Millie and Uncle Arthur. The others were given less agrarian chores.

INTO THE DARKNESS

A month after my father's pet monkey, Chico, left by court order (more about him later), the family was dealt a life-changing blow. Gi had lost his pet and was about to lose his father. In June 1916, the BMT West End Line opened, extending the El from 9th Avenue to

18th Avenue, darkening 30th Street to 86th Street. My father's family lived near 61st Street, off 11th Avenue, not far from where the El made a sharp and noisy turn. (Later on, Grandma lived with Aunt Millie on 67th Street, between 14th and 15th avenues, the only place I remember.) At the same time the El was going up, Domenico De Simone, at the age of 40, died suddenly.

One story was that he was struck on the head by a block of ice that fell from a roof. Another report was that he was struck by a bullet while fleeing the police during those times when the infamous La Mano Nera—the "Black Hand" extortion racket— ruled the neighborhoods. Another source mentioned hemophilia. Whatever the cause of death, he was gone, leaving a widow with 6 small children.

The construction of the El separated the neighborhood forever. The El did not run directly in front of the De Simone farm, but it was close enough, and so my father grew up in its shadow, a shadow that cloaked poverty and despair, and sometimes the truth. The only thing that was permitted to shine was pride, the deadly sin disguised as a shield, which became the mask for the entire clan during the bad times.

The De Simones became a viciously proud cast of storytellers and magicians, able to substitute tales for reality. For anyone who had the nerve to ask a personal question, a De Simone was able to, in an instant, transform with flowery words their sow's ear subsistence into a lovely silk purse joyride.

Aunt Millie once told me that she had unexpected company one morning, and she made them coffee in china cups, and she scraped the mold off the bread and served it with butter and jam on a lovely plate. The table setting looked like brunch being served at a palace. That's how it's done.

THE COURTSHIP OF ANTONIO'S DAUGHTER

Written in the most elegant script on my mother's birth certificate was her name, Francesca Giovanna Ferro. That was as close to elegance as she would ever get. Everyone knew her as Frances Joan, and there went the lyrical grace of the name. She was born on May 10, 1917, in a time when our country's women were birthing the greatest generation of Americans. These were the men and women that contributed their young adulthood to the great cause of WWII, whether it was in battle overseas, or here at home.

My mother did her patriotic part by making propellers for fighter planes in a machine plant that was converted from a bookbinding factory. She was a veritable Rosie the Riveter. Everyone did his or her part, for the mission was clear: rid the world of A.H. and Party, along with his Japanese partners. Italy was an associate of theirs for a time, but my family chose to forget that. When questioned about Benito Mussolini, someone in the family would always boast, in his defense, that he cleaned up Italy. Whatever the hell that means!

My father was born on December 1, 1908, which made him too young to serve in World War I, and when The Big One began, he was classified 4F because of a bleeding ulcer, so he never had his shot Over There. He was already in his 30s when he had tried 3 times to enlist for WWII (to my mother's distress) and was turned down each time (to my mother's glee). He stayed over here. His service to our country was to comfort the ladies left behind.

In his heyday back in the late 1920s, Blackie, as he was known to his friends, was an accomplished ballroom dancer, the winner of several trophies. My father even danced a close 2nd to George Raft, before Raft bolero-ed his way into the movies. Blackie's charm, dark good looks, and outrageously dry sense of humor had women dancing well after the music stopped. He inherited his mother's bedroom eyes, and they served him well in many boudoirs.

Blackie got his name from a foreman at a trucking company when he was about 12. He was so tanned from loading trucks that he looked "black." The name stuck, but to the family, he was always Gi. He gave up loading trucks and other strenuous work when he got his driver's license and drove a cab in New York City, a career that lasted 47 years.

In 1925, my mother's family moved from a rat- and roach-infested tenement apartment on Mott Street in Manhattan to the promised land—Brooklyn. My grandfather Antonio was running a profitable trash carting business and wanted his family to have a better life. Their house in Brooklyn (on 78th Street off New Utrecht Avenue, a stone's throw from the El) was in what was called a "mixed" area. In those days, the mix was Italian and Jewish. Right next door to their house was the Imperial Mansion, a kosher catering hall. Frances became practically fluent in Yiddish, learning the language from the staff. Later on, the kosher was dropped and it became the Imperial Terrace, catering to all.

Frances must have had wonderful memories of that time in her life, because one of the last things she said before she died was that she wished she could have lived in that house on 78th Street forever. And, for the traditional post-funeral last ride past one's house, she requested that we drive past the home she loved, and not where she died. My father had won plenty of money playing poker and betting on the ponies—enough to buy several houses for her, including the happy home from her childhood—but it just wasn't in the cards.

In 1931, Francesca met Giuseppe for the first time, sort of. She was 14 and known as Frances. It was a common practice in the public schools to anglicize Italian names, if it hadn't been done on Ellis Island already. Filomena became Phyllis, Luisa became Louise, Giovanni was called John, and Silvestri was changed to Caesar (don't ask!). I even know a Mariano that was renamed Morris.

My father, 23, had already been married and divorced by the time he was 20, and he was making pretty good money as a cab driver and part-time gambler. He drove a very fancy 1930 Cord Auburn.

He had seen my mother many times and was smitten with her creamy white complexion, natural snowy blonde hair, and bright blue eyes. But it was her smile that did him in. Frances had the most incredible dimples when she smiled. Sadly, as the years went on, she had less and less to smile about, and those gorgeous dimples became haggard lifelines.

Blackie made it his campaign to wait for her after school, parking his fancy car in front of Shallow Junior High School in Bensonhurst every day, for weeks. As she walked home, he'd drive slowly and call out to her to offer her a ride. She always refused, telling him to get lost. Her rebuffs intrigued Blackie. He tried again.

"Get lost!"

And still again, on his Harley Davidson motorcycle.

"Get lost!"

He even took a chance without the machinery and asked if he could walk her home.

"Get lost!"

She's a spunky one, he thought, but he was also a bit bewildered. There wasn't a girl in Brooklyn who didn't want to go for a ride with Blackie...and maybe even more! All the women loved him. What was it about

Frances? What made her different? He had to change his strategy.

One day, he showed up at the house on 78th Street. My grandfather Antonio answered Blackie's knock at the door. Blackie was very respectful when he asked Signore Ferro if he could "keep company" with Frances. Grandpa gave him a knock on the head and went back in the house. While Blackie retreated to his car, he heard a voice behind him yelling in Italian.

"Che vuoi con mia figlia? Ella é una bambina. Tu sei un'uomo grande. Vatene, o mazateti!" (What do you want with my daughter? She's a little girl. You're a grown man. Get out of here, or I'll kill you!)

Then, Blackie noticed the shotgun. He hit the gas of his Cord Auburn and took off. Grandpa was still shouting and waving the gun, even when Blackie's car was out of sight.

"Get lost, you bum!"

My mother witnessed the incident from the parlor window and laughed like hell. Actually, Frances had a wild crush on Blackie, but she refused to be like those other foolish girls falling at this feet. Like her mother, Emelia, she had all intentions of holding on to her precious jewel until a gold wedding band was on her finger.

When Frances turned 16, Grandpa allowed her to keep company with Gi. This meant that he could sit in the parlor and have a glass of homemade wine or a cup of espresso. They sat on opposite sides of the room. What her protective father (and mother) didn't know was that Frances had been playing hooky for a year, taking rides on the Harley and in Gi's fancy car. She refused to call him Blackie and opted to call him Gi, as his family called him. He only tried to go past the chaste "so long" kiss once, and Frances nearly knocked him to the ground.

"Not till you put a ring on my finger!"

This restrained courtship continued. Blackie had no problem bedding down women, so he was patient with Frances while taking care of business elsewhere. (My father spent six months in jail in 1927 accused of statutory rape by a girl that said the baby she was carrying was his. The blood test proved otherwise, and the unfortunate girl broke down in tears when she was told, like in an early version of *Montel*. She confessed that she only said that because she loved him and wanted to marry him. Whose baby was it? No idea! The charges were dismissed.)

Sometime in 1938, Grandpa gave his very vocal disappointing permission for them to marry. It was a lost cause. Frances didn't want anyone else. So, would Antonio be stuck with supporting a spinster? Her older sisters already had kids, having both married at the ripe age of 18. Better she should marry than have that lonely fate of living with relatives. He figured, if she wants him, she can have him. The bed they make, she will just have to lie in it...even cry in it.

Frances didn't start the crying for a few years. Theirs was an exciting, fun-packed ride—in cars, on motorcycles, with surprise gifts and with dancing. My mother was possessive, to say the least. She once dragged a woman out of a dance hall, by her hair, and left her on the sidewalk.

"He's with me! Look at him again that way, and you'll really see what I'm made of."

Blackie ate it up!

For their first real date involving family as an engaged couple, Blackie took Frances to meet his mother and his siblings for a Sunday dinner. My grandmother asked her if she smoked. Frances didn't lie but explained that it would be improper to smoke in front of the family. Grandma told her to "fug" the family and have a cigarette. Even before dinner made it to the table, Blackie gave Frances a peck on the cheek and left, telling her he'd be right back. He showed up 6 hours later. My mother told him, as she made the sign of the cross (which meant her statement is written in stone), that she would never, ever have another meal at his mother's house. And, she never did.

There was no doubt that Blackie truly didn't want to get married, but on September 30, 1939, after a 6-year courtship, in the company of the entire family and with the shotgun in plain view as a sign of Grandpa's protest, Frances and Gi were married in a civil ceremony at City Hall in Brooklyn, New York. Aunt Josie and Uncle Ceasar stood up as maid of honor and best man.

Frances wanted a church wedding, but the priest told her that the Catholic Church didn't marry divorced people. It didn't matter that my father was married for less than a year, 10 years earlier. Father O'Reilly also told her that she should come back in 7 years for a blessing so that her children, should she have any, would not be considered bastards. She never went back for the blessing—never went back to church at all—concluding that Blackie would be no less divorced in 7 years, or even 100 years.

At the proper time, when my brothers and I were able to understand, she told us, her 3 little bastards, what she really thought. The Catholic Church was run by a bunch of hypocrites who ate chicken on Fridays (and called it fowl, not meat), had an offensive "do as I say, but not as I do" policy, were probably not celibate, and, finally, that if we didn't go to Mass every Sunday and finish catechism classes, she'd break our legs. She believed in God, not the church.

CHAPTER TWO
EL AMENITIES

Life under the El was different from living *around the corner*. In more upscale neighborhoods, some would say that the spot where the El meets *around the corner* could be described as Dysfunction Junction. *Around the corner*, they had birds like sparrows and robins and starlings fluttering about that perched happily on telephone poles and clotheslines.

We had birds flying around, just like they did, but ours were dark, large-winged, bug-eyed, slow-moving creatures that hung from the steel beams of the El, by their feet. Our birds were bats. Yet, *around the corner*, there were one and 2-family houses that had small but tended lawns and colorful bushes and plants in the front yards—roses, tulips, daffodils. If it's true that a tree grows in Brooklyn, it didn't grow on my street.

On the windowsills that faced the El, my mother had plastic geraniums in plastic pots that were meant to be redemptive and defiant little red patches against the steely gray background. We were, however, able to raise snake plants on the fire escape, which my mother, who marveled at anything that grew from a seed, said could survive in a closet. Apparently, so could we, because we were raised, like those snake plants, out of the sun, away from the light...under the El.

When I was little, my mother would take me on "field trips" down the block to her friend Mary Tuorto's house to stand outside her fence and admire the flowers. Frances would describe each flower and almost weep at their beauty. Of all, she loved red roses.

It's worth noting that Frances had the greenest thumb. She could drop a paper clip in some dirt, and a tree of clips would grow. I always felt bad that she never had a real garden to tend to. I was, however, pleased to hear from a psychic that Frances was in heaven living in a little house with a garden filled with plump red roses. Gotta believe in something!

When you are born under the El, the world is dark and noisy. But I never knew that. I thought everyone fell asleep to the sound of a train screeching by. It was an urban lullaby. We also learned very early that during conversations, we had to stop mid-sentence, wait until the train passed outside our windows, and only then resume talking. There was no way to hear each other over the piercing sound of metal wheels on steel tracks. The television volume was raised to the level of air raid warning because it was too much trouble, in those long ago days before remote controls, to get up, walk 2 steps to the television, and adjust the volume to accommodate the train schedule.

NO PLAZA SUITE FOR US

We lived above a false-teeth laboratory in a railroad-style apartment, where you were able to see the entire thing from either end. (While I use the word "style," the only thing that can be said of its style was that it was designed to be indoors and had a roof.) It was a cold water flat (that means no running hot water), and the kitchen, at one end and off to the left, permitted one person at a time to occupy its small space. In it was a double sink—one side was for dishes, and the other, called the tub, was deep enough for a scrub board and used for washing clothes (and babies). No washing machine for us. The advantage to having just cold water was the privilege of drinking the best tasting and coldest water in the world. Somebody should have bottled it.

Here's how laundry day went: first, we'd wet the clothes in the icy water under the faucet in the sink. Next, we'd soap each article of clothing with a bar of lye soap and then scrape the clothes against the washboard, turn the garments over, slam them against the board, repeat several times until each part of the garbs got a good beating—especially the underwear—rinse them under more running cold water, and finally wring them out. My mother had to do that part for me. I was a lousy wringer. After the thrashing and strangling, the clothes were sentenced to a hanging, where they were lined up to dry on a clothesline in a communal courtyard amid a cloud of soot. It was only in cold weather that these crimeless victims were able to stand up for themselves, when they were taken in, stiff and freezing.

We ironed everything. The clothes were dampened with a sprinkler bottle, rolled up, and put in the refrigerator for several hours. We were lucky to have an ironing board; however, my mother taught me how to iron on a towel on the table. I still have the skill to iron anywhere—tables, floors, countertops.

The iron we used was called a dry iron—no steam… hence the sprinkling. And, there was no such thing as "permanent press." Each piece that made its way from the scrub board to the ironing board was ironed. Times have changed.

And, back to the tub. Yes, babies were also scrubbed in the tub with the same lye soap. The only difference was, they weren't grated against the board or wrung out and hung on the clothesline.

The bath towel, used by everyone, stayed in the bathroom. The dishtowel, known to us as the *moppina*, was used to wipe babies, slightly. Mostly, the kids air dried, so their pajamas looked glued on. The *moppina* served as the family napkin, tissue, hand towel, and whatever else needed a quick rub. We passed it around until it stunk. Nobody ever got sick.

Next to the sink was a cupboard in the wall called a dumb waiter, which had been used in the past to carry small freight from one floor to another and to the basement. It had been converted into a mini pantry, its dumb waiting days long gone.

The apartment had some charm, I guess. Its tin ceilings with art deco patterns are now back in fashion, and the nouveau riche will pay handsomely for them. We also had crown molding—before it was characterized as a big plus in houses—in every room, painted with high gloss enamel paint, which I am sure contained plenty of lead. All the walls were papered in flowery patterns to cover the cracked plasterboard. Add the European shower (which I write about later), and we were so chic, we didn't know it.

The entire place was on a pronounced slant. The pictures were hung straight, so the frames looked crooked, and that gave the place a Willy Wonka ambiance. Since the floor was slanted, if we had soup, it sat in the bowl at an angle. The only times the slant helped was when Richard and I would play marbles in the main entrance, which we generously called the foyer. We had better rolls on the sloped linoleum.

There was a huge black cast iron water heater smack in the center of the kitchen, and hanging from its side was a box of long wooden matches. When other parents were warning their children of the dangers of playing with matches, my mother was reminding us to light the water heater. (I started at 3!) If we forgot, we had no hot water for washing clothes or dishes, or for us to take a bath. I say "a bath"—singular—because we never had enough hot water for more than one bath a day. Even when we remembered to light the heater, it took several hours to get enough water to fill the giant clawfoot bathtub. Our chic family only took a bath once a week—maybe.

Since there were 5 of us (sometimes, when Blackie showed up), we had sponge baths on a regular basis, standing on a towel (not the *moppina*) at the bathroom sink. We had to plug the drain with an old washcloth and then fill the sink with hot water (when we remembered). We used a medicinal-smelling brown soap—could have been the lye soap, not sure—to quickly wash the body's essentials, and then we emptied the soapy water and promptly rinsed off before the hot water ran out. If the hot water ran out, so did our luck. Cold water it was.

As I mentioned, the bathtub was one of those long, deep, porcelain kinds with claw-footed legs. We also had a rubber hose hooked up to the spout, which was used to quickly rinse off before the water turned cold. Today, the wealthy and glamorous attach a shiny brass or gold-plated tube to the faucet and call it a European shower. I never knew how ahead of our time we were. (At least we had a bathtub in its own room. Some apartments had, and still have, the tub in the kitchen.)

The tub took up most of the bathroom. It was easy to burn your ass on the steam pipe just turning to hang the rubber hose or flush the toilet. Sometimes, I was able to fill the tub with enough hot water and prepare to spend 15 soothing minutes soaking my entire body, a change from the sponge quickie. But always, at the last minute, my brother Richard would dance around outside the bathroom doing the "I have to pee" jig and the "I'll only be a minute" chant. I'd fall for that gag every time and let him go in first. And without fail, the next sound we heard was the splash of a body hitting the water.

"He stole my bath water!"

Every single time. I was really stupid.

The bedrooms faced the El, so the blinds were always kept shut. It wasn't as if we were blocking any light, for any lighting we had came from the 25-watt bulb above the pull chain on the ceiling. We kept the blinds closed because the passengers on the train could see right into our apartment, and my mother didn't want to give everybody a "free show." It became a matter of "we can see them, but they can't see us."

To further embellish the sleeping arrangements, my brother Joseph started his life sleeping in a crib at the foot of my parents' bed. He graduated at some point to a bed that folds in half, fastened by metal clasps, or as we called it, an *abranda*, the slang Italian word for daybed. In the morning, it was folded and pushed to a corner of the room, where it didn't quite fit. We all managed to stub our toe on the *abranda* all the time.

Under the master bed (the master refers to the bed, because the master himself wasn't in it every night) was a porcelain piss pot, or *pishadoo*, so my father wouldn't have to take the walk to the toilet in the middle of the night.

In the morning, my mother would yell from the kitchen, "Somebody, empty the piss pot!"

That's when we'd try to hide and hope Frances would get tired of chasing us and do the deed herself. Richard told me that when Blackie came home from work at 3:00 a.m., he'd wake Richard up and have him pee in the pot, then send him back to bed. This was done to help prevent Richard from wetting the bed. I never knew Richard was a bed-wetter, and we slept in the same bed!

Richard and I slept in a tiny triangular room off to the side of another small room belonging to my parents. The window in the triangle room was set at a sharp angle, which could have been a visual aid in a geometry class. We slept in the same single bed, head-to-feet. His feet were in my face, and they stunk. I kept my feet dangling slightly off the bed.

When my mother observed that I started sprouting at about 9 years old, the head-to-foot arrangement ended. Richard was 12. We found each other revolting, so we had managed to never touch, not even elbows, for all that time. That first move into my "becoming a lady" got me the triangle room to myself, and Richard was moved into the windowless middle room. That was after Grandma died, and her bed was removed, and he slept on a high-riser (sometimes called a trundle bed because of the pullout bed underneath).

Many years later, the television on a stand was moved in there from the all-purpose room (it wasn't that we wanted to be in the same room, you know, like a family—we had no choice) leaving absolutely no floor space. We literally had to climb over the TV to get to the high-riser. Oh, yes, and for added eye candy, there was a stick lamp stuck in the corner next to the bed.

The apartment was a virtual eat-in dormitory. The dining room was what I guess would now be called the family room, or an all-purpose room. There was a Formica table trimmed in ridged chrome and chrome chairs with red leatherette seats and backs, which were rimmed with chrome studs (very retro...now!). It was the place where we ate, argued, watched TV, did our homework, and, in the evenings, helped my mother do her "homework"—making key chains for extra money. She got paid a penny a piece.

My mother was quick with her fingers; she had to

be quick at those wages. I remember vividly the click, click, click against the table as the key chains piled up. The clicking lasted well into the night, as her cigarette butts piled up in the ashtray and the smell of muddy coffee permeated the apartment.

At the end of each week, Richard and I counted and bagged the key chains, and then one of us brought them to a woman named Nettie, who lived in a semi-attached house *around the corner*. She didn't need the money, so she didn't do the work. She farmed out the work and took her cut. We'd wait for Nettie in her carpeted, fancy-draped, festooned, cornice-boarded dining room. A real dining room. We'd watch Nettie tally up the key chains on her sturdy and heavily carved mahogany dining room table. Then, she'd give us the bounty to bring back to my mother—usually about 7 or 8 dollars.

EIGHTY-EIGHT KEYS OFFER A RESPITE

One wall of our dining room was reserved for my mother's prized possession, an old player piano. We didn't have drapes. We used to have café curtains that Frances bought from a man we called "the Jew" (more about that horrid reference later). But, they hung too close to the gas heater, and one night, they caught fire. It was one of those rare occasions that my father was actually home all night, and he saved our lives.

I never knew where the piano came from. I only know that it took 3 men to get it up the stairs, through the slanted foyer, and planted next to the wall. The "player" part of the piano didn't work at all, and the piano itself was slightly out of tune, but my mother loved that piano and taught herself to play.

Everyone used to say, "Just hum something—

Frances will find the right keys."

Frances sat at that piano and, with her squatty fingers, tested the black and whites until she was satisfied—then she played familiar melodies, and the rest of us joined in, singing.

Sometimes, a little sunshine seeps through, even if you live in the dark. This was one of the bright spots, singing songs and seeing a very rare smile on my mother's face. We'd begin with a ditty:

> Six o'clock this morning,
> Miss Murphy came around
> With a slice of bread and butter
> That weighed a half a pound.
> The coffee tastes like tobacco juice,
> The bread was hard and stale,
> And that's the way they fed the bums
> In the Richmond County jail.
> The bed bugs and the roaches
> Were havin' a game of ball;
> The bed bugs lost, lost their head,
> And nearly threw me out of bed.
> Shave and a haircut, two bits!

Then, my father, who made occasional cameo appearances, would sing an old number. As a child, I knew I never wanted to be that girl in the song:

> You're the kind of a girl that men forget,
> Just a toy to enjoy for a while,
> But when men settle down,
> They always find an old fashioned girl,
> With an old fashioned smile.
> You will soon realize
> That you're not so wise
> When the years bring you tears of regret,

For when they play
'Here Comes the Bride'
You'll stand outside—
You're the girl that men forget.

My mother would add at the end, "Remember, a man won't buy the cow if he gets the milk for free!"

While other young girls were swooning over the likes of Elvis and Fabian, I enjoyed Sinatra, Perry Como, and Mario Lanza, and I sang along with Rosemary Clooney and Sarah Vaughan, and Gershwin's music. My favorite was Cole Porter's "My Heart Belongs to Daddy," made popular by the wonderful Mary Martin. Frances played, and I sang the lyrics directly to my father. I didn't realize at the time that "Daddy" didn't mean father, and "My Heart" did not belong to a little girl singing to her papa. It was really about a girl that men forget. But it didn't matter. I sang the song to my daddy, the man who had my heart.

SATURDAY NIGHT FERVOR

Blackie was never home on Saturdays—work or women or a poker game, take your pick. The Saturday night ritual was ice cream, the newspapers, and *Your Show of Shows*. One of us had to go to the candy store, which was around the corner and five long blocks away, to get the ice cream and newspapers and get back in time for Sid Caesar and Imogene Coca. My mother gave us just enough money to buy four ice cream cones and three newspapers. Sometimes, if she ate some of the hot cherry peppers she kept hanging from the clothesline in the kitchen (the longer they hung there, the hotter they got), she'd add another three cents for a small cup of Coca-Cola syrup, a sure-fire remedy for heartburn and stomach aches.

The man behind the ice cream counter was also named Sid. He had quite a show of his own going. Sid's left arm was missing up to just above his elbow, leaving a stump protruding from his shoulder, where the sleeve of his shirt was pinned. There were numbers printed across the wrist of his right hand. I had seen numbers like this on our upstairs neighbor.

The stump presented no challenge at all to Sid. He'd simply shove the cone under his short arm so that the cone stuck out sideways; then, he'd scoop up the ice cream and push it into the cone. There were occasional mishaps when the ice cream wasn't pushed down tight enough, or when one of the cones would slide out of his sweaty armpit and have to be replaced.

But Sid took this in stride, shrugging and smiling. "Oy vey, lost another one. What can you do?"

We'd laugh along with him and try not to think that we were about to eat an ice cream cone that smelled like Sid's armpit. Sid was probably happy to be flinging ice cream or dropping anything at all, far away from the people who took his left arm and tattooed a permanent reminder on his right one.

I loved Saturday nights, especially when it wasn't my turn to schlep around the corner and trudge those five long blocks with the Sunday editions of the *Daily News*, the *Daily Mirror*, and the *Herald Tribune* under one arm and a bag of melting ice cream cones under the other. By the time I'd get home and my mother had opened the bag, the ice cream cones looked like one blob of merging colors with four brown dunce caps sticking up out of it. We separated the blobs as best we could, salvaging our own flavors: butter pecan for Frances, Joseph's cherry vanilla, plain vanilla for Richard, and I always had chocolate with sprinkles. The papers had to be reorganized because I'd drop them at least a dozen times on the way.

Rainy nights were the worst. But nothing dampened those evenings. We'd sit in the multi-purpose room on the linoleum floor, in a semi-circle around the tiny screen TV (a secondhand set from my aunt Louise), and watch a snowy version of *Your Show of Shows*, slurping our ice cream cones voraciously before they melted completely. It was a sticky mess. Oh, but, what a lovely mess it was.

When the family (aunts, uncles, and cousins) visited on Sundays, it was terrific. If we looked out the window after hearing a train go by, we could see some of them descend the steps of the 79th Street stop.

After all the greetings were done, and we were ready to eat, there was always the call from someone to "put up the water!" and when the water was boiled, "throw the macs!" (boil the water for the pasta and toss in the pasta). After dinner at 3:00 p.m., once we'd had fruit and nuts, pastries (compliments of Aunt Tillie and Uncle Jack, owners of Luigi Alba Pastry Shop), cheesecake, and some other sweets, the Pokeno game hit the table.

I would give anything to see my aunts and uncles again crowding the table, fishing for pennies, and calling out the cards.

"Jack of spades!"

And there was always a mistake.

"No, John, that's the jack of clubs!"

Poor Uncle John. He could barely read or write, and since he was my mother's brother—no blood relation to Blackie—card playing was not his gig. He had a steady job as a night watchman at the Brooklyn Navy Yard.

Blackie even joined in to play Pokeno on Sunday evenings when he was around. I think he thought the whole thing silly after playing poker for hundreds, even thousands of dollars. But, his presence increased the energy of the game, and the laughs increased, too, by hundreds, even thousands. And, he sang songs while the others contemplated their odds of winning 12 cents.

When someone took too long to play their hand, he belted out Irving Berlin's song, *"I'm all alone, by the telephone, waiting for a ring, a ting-a-ling..."*

Sometimes, Aunt Louise (my favorite aunt, and the one everyone says I look like) would call from Kansas City to say hello to her sisters and brothers, and Blackie would do another rendition of the song, or sing to her over the phone, *"I'll be loving you, always..."*

On or about 7:00 p.m., the food was hauled out again, or my mother made a pizza from dough she bought at Modica's bakery around the corner on 17th Avenue. Italian families always mistake a deep breath for hunger, so we ate again. Us kids usually spent the day jumping on my mother's bed, or outside, chasing each other, or playing "hit the stick," or "kick the can," or "it"—outdoor games that required no devices, just arms, legs and a little imagination...or maybe a ball.

AN EL-DEFINED CHRISTMAS

Evening festivities at Christmas time started out nicely for us. Frances waited until late Christmas Eve, when she was sure to get a bargain on a puny pine, to haggle with the bundled-up, freezing Jewish guy who sold the trees.

She'd argue, "You're only going to burn them now. It's Christmas Eve. Why not make the 50 cents? It's better than nothing."

So, every year, we had the not-so-cream-of-the-crop Christmas tree, always with the sparse side facing the wall. We had very few ornaments, but the silver icicles (which we called tinsel) were cheap. On that O

Holy Night, it was the job of her 3 bastard children to throw the tinsel at the tree until it looked like slivered steel that was leftover from the El. My mother had a Victrola that played '78 records that she'd plug in by the front window to blast the neighborhood and El train passengers with Christmas songs.

Frances got real hip in the sixties when she bought a silver tree, thereby putting the tinsel out of business. She decorated it with blue glass balls. Behind it, on the floor, was an electric rotating wheel that made the tree glisten in primary colors. It was not a beautiful sight— nothing resembling a winter wonderland. In fact, it was cold, icy, and killed some of the rare warmth in our cold water flat. It just about ruined Christmas for the 3 bastards.

When Grandma was with us, Christmas Eve dinner was a fish festival: eels swimming in the bathtub before they were slaughtered and sautéed; *polpo* (octopus), calamari, and linguine with clam sauce; whiting salad (delicious flaked fish with black olives drizzled with olive oil); fried shrimp and flounder; my mother's great rice balls. And, of course, bread—loaves and loaves of bread. I think Uncle Rico paid for most of it, and no doubt Uncle Ceasar, too. What a feast! Too bad I only ate the bread.

I don't remember Blackie ever being home on Christmas Eve...he'd arrive in the middle of the night, like a tardy Santa, only without the bag of goodies.

In 1953, on my birthday, my mother took me (and baby Joseph, I think) to see Santa at Macy's. The 8th floor at Macy's rivaled Santa's North Pole workshop. It was a wonder. As a child who had approached her 5th birthday, it was magical. And, there was Santa on his throne. Unlike the famous holiday movie, *A Christmas Story*, where kids were kicked down a slide, my Santa was sweet.

I asked him for a walking doll as tall as I, and a piano. When we got home, there they were! The doll was sitting on the bed in my (and Richard's) room, and the piano was next to the dresser. Blackie was there in the middle of the afternoon. I was thinking that I was the luckiest little girl in the world, and wow, Santa was amazing. He didn't even wait for Christmas. He gave me what I wanted on my birthday! Then, I heard my parents trying to whisper.

"Gi, why did you buy them today? I already ordered them for Christmas."

My father replied, "Geez, Frances, I just wanted her to have them for her birthday."

The piano order was cancelled, but another doll arrived the next day. Either Santa messed up, or he thought I was such a good little girl, he gave me *two* dolls. Of course, Santa had nothing to do with it, and that was the year I stopped believing in him. We should never stop believing.

HOT SUMMERS AND FAMILY BONDS

In the summer of 1960, we had a little bit of excitement when JFK and Jackie rode along New Utrecht Avenue in a convertible. We could practically touch the dynamic presidential candidate and his lovely pregnant wife. Frances tried to get close to their car but was almost run over by a Secret Service car, forcing her to throw herself on a parked car, doing something she hated...giving the onlookers a free show!

When she recovered, her only remark was, "She has a lot of freckles."

Summers were hot under the El. Sometimes, we opened the windows on both sides of the apartment, in the bedroom and the dining room, to get some cross ventilation going. But breezes only happened when a train went by faster than usual, and normally, those were the empty trains on their way to the depot. The occasional breezes carried in the black molecules of soot—we could even smell it. Most of the time, we just suffocated and put cold, wet rags on our pulse points every 10 minutes or so (my mother's invention) to get some relief.

On particularly stifling nights, my brothers and I took turns sleeping on a mattress out on the fire escape. Who cared that the fire escapes faced the courtyard (maybe it was really an air shaft) and that we were on display for the neighbors? It was cooler than the apartment, and for us, it was like camping. Of course, below us, beneath the fire escape, was the abyss—the courtyard, dark and gloomy. But if we kept our eyes shut, we had fun. Inside, my mother continued the cold rag routine, freshening the rags every few hours in the bathroom sink.

Many evenings after dinner were spent on the roof, or Tar Beach, as we called it. Frances generally brought a pitcher of ice water for drinking and a bucket of cold water for the rags. We'd sit on a blanket and watch the fireworks show from Coney Island, or just watch the sun go down on the world *around the corner*. Sometimes, my aunts and uncles joined us up there, usually on Sundays after the second round of macaroni and meatballs, or pizza, and following a few confused games of Pokeno. They sat around and sang Italian songs. It started with something upbeat, like "Lazy Mary," and ended, without fail, with the heart-tugging "Mama."

> When the evening shadows fall,
> And a lovely day is through,
> With longing I recall

The days I spent with you...
Until that day when we're together once more,
I live in these memories,
Until we're together once more...
O, Mama...

All the songs were sung in Italian, and even if you didn't understand a word, it was wonderful. My mother and her brothers and sisters would glance at one another through misty eyes. Their silent memories filled the air.

Tar Beach was too hot during the day. The sun beating down on the black tar was unbearable. My aunt Phylly (née Filomena, aka Phyllis) lived four houses down, on the top floor in the last of the pie-shaped buildings where under the El meets *around the corner*. Her apartment cut the sharpest angle, shaping her front room into an acute triangle.

Sometimes, in the morning, before any of us were dressed, Aunt Phylly would call out from her bathroom window, the only one of her windows that faced the courtyard, and ask my mother for a cup of milk, or sugar, or whatever. Aunt Phylly's apartment had lots of natural light, courtesy of *around the corner*, but there was nothing courteous about Phylly's welcome.

"Send Joanne by the roof," she would say.

I'd run across the roof to Aunt Phylly's as fast as I could, praying I would not sink into the sticky, scalding tar.

At age 9, I had my first cigarette on Tar Beach. I stole one of my mother's non-filtered Camels, lit it, inhaled, and nearly fell off the roof. I didn't have another cigarette until I was 14, when my father handed me one of his filtered L&Ms. I was sitting at the dining room table, so I was able to handle the dizziness. My father told me I looked very grown up. My mother was furious, pointing out that she'd consent to my smoking only at 16, which she considered the appropriate age to start killing yourself.

When Richard saw me with the cigarette, he took a fit. "She's too young! I had to wait until I was 16."

I also had my first kiss on the tar, which was much better than smoking.

Sometimes, I'd go up on the roof alone and look out at the world beyond the El, far away from *around the corner*, and pick out the house I wanted to live in when I grew up. Or, I'd wonder, in what direction was Kansas City? Could my aunt Louise see me from that far away? I hoped she knew that I wished that she and my cousin Bobby never moved away.

PETS AND OTHER GUESTS

In the late 1950s, the rent for our tiny 5-room cold water flat under the El was 30 dollars a month. The mice, roaches, water bugs, and various species of spiders didn't pay rent, but they had the run of the place. My mother thought we were getting robbed at 30 a month, so she called the OPA, an organization that regulated rents, and an investigator was sent. When the investigator left, he was shaking off his clothes, which, no doubt, he burned at first opportunity. Our rent was reduced to 26 dollars a month. The 4-buck reprieve was for the uninvited occupants and the lack of hot water.

A favorite hangout for water bugs was the bathroom, and this made using the facilities an adventure for the whole family. None of us ever read newspapers or magazines on the john—nor did we call it John, a name that, for us, was always followed by The Baptist. We never called it the throne either, because there was nothing royal about sitting on a cold opening with your underwear around your ankles. It was the can. And, furthermore, it was a can of bugs, bugs on steroids. Those water bugs were fast. There was a consistent sound of a shoe hitting the floor.

Bang, "Shit!" Bang, bang, "Shit...got him!"

One morning, I was ironing a dress for school when out of nowhere, a water bug waddled across the ironing board. Usually, they ran swiftly, but this one must have been arthritic. Overcome with revulsion, I picked up the hot iron, aimed it, and dropped it squarely on the water bug. I scorched and crushed the little bugger, simultaneously. It was not pretty; in fact, the sight of the black bug stuck to the bottom of the iron made me sick. It was my mother who scraped off the remains, a job that I am sure is not listed in the Mother Manual.

Eventually, the bug business became a game, so we named them. Mice were Mickeys, water bugs were Wallys, and roaches were Ronalds.

"Ma, Mickey's drinking your coffee." She'd reply, "Don't worry, the caffeine will kill him."

"There's a Ronald in my Corn Flakes." She'd suggest, "Throw the whole thing down the sink and have toast."

"Wally's swimming in my bath water." She'd say, "Scoop him out, the water's still good."

We did, sometimes, have real pets, but they never seemed to last long. The parakeets were always found feet up in just a few days. Perhaps we should have hung the cage away from the gas radiator. One parakeet, Sofia, survived the gas but flew into a wall and fell to the floor like a stone. Maybe she was high from the gas.

Joseph had a chicken he named Charlie. Joseph kept Charlie on a leash and proudly took him for walks around the corner and down the block to what we called "the dirt park," next to "the swing park" that had monkey bars, seesaws, and swings. Until I was about 10, there was a house from the Revolutionary War that sat on the dirt park. We were sure it was haunted and convinced that George Washington slept there.

Charlie the Chicken had to live on the roof because Frances said chickens liked to be outside. Joseph made a house for him out of an orange crate and fed him oatmeal. Early one morning, we heard a systematic series of cock-a-doodle-doo's. The neighbors were furious, and Charlie had to go.

One day, I brought home a crate of baby chicks, and Frances lost her mind. "They can't stay here. They have to go grow up in a warm place."

"Where?"

"The chicken farm."

The "chicken farm" in our neighborhood was the slaughterhouse on 18th Avenue. We could hear them screaming when they got plump enough to be polished off and plucked. And, you could smell the place for miles.

We once had a dog named Brownie that shared his birthday with me and Blackie—well, his name was on the cake.

One time, Blackie woke us all up in the middle of the night. He brought home a monkey. It was adorable, swinging from the light fixture and running all over the place. Blackie wanted to keep it. We wanted to keep it.

My mother chain smoked 5 cigarettes. "It can't stay here, Gi! It will crap all over!"

Blackie left and came back a little while later sans monkey, which surely brought back a memory from his childhood.

When my father was about 8 years old, he had a pet monkey named Chico. I don't know where the monkey came from, and no one would have cared. No one would have even noticed, since the farm was fenced in and had very few visitors. It was like having a pet dog. Chico was at my father's side or sitting on his shoulder all through the day, and sometimes, he helped clean up the barn floor. I'm sure that was hilarious to watch.

At night, Chico slept on a blanket on the floor next to Gi's bed. On Sunday mornings, when Gi slept late, Chico would sit on the fence that faced the street. The street they lived on was the direct route to St. Rosalia's Church, and the neighborhood Italian dowagers took that route every Sunday. Some of them went to Mass every day, just as my grandmother Francesca did.

On one particular Sunday, one of the ladies in black noticed something peculiar. Chico was sitting on the fence, snorting, with a full, toothy smile on his face. One hand was cradling the back of his head in a somewhat cheesecake pose; his other hand was wrapped around his penis, joyfully playing with himself.

One of the old ladies almost fainted dead away in the street. "We will put a stop to this!"

After mass, all three dried prunes descended on my grandmother and told her that the monkey had to go! She told them that she would keep the monkey away from the fence and that Chico was a working monkey, a big help around the place. The old women were not satisfied. They went directly to the police. No one was arrested, but my grandmother had to appear in court to explain all the manual labors of Chico the monkey.

Francesca pleaded with the judge by way of an Italian interpreter while 8-year-old Gi sat in a chair, holding on to Chico. The judge ruled that Chico was better off living in a zoo with creatures of his own kind. He allowed my father to take the ride with Chico in the police motorcycle sidecar all the way to the Bronx Zoo.

My father told us this story a million times, and a million times he cried when he got to the part where the police officers, though kind, had to pry Chico from him, and how he sobbed as he watched Chico and the cops go through the zoo's gate, and how he sobbed until Chico was out of sight. He told us that he cried for weeks.

When I was 9, I found a tiny white kitten in the gutter and brought it home. The poor little thing died within an hour from the gas fumes. I cried and cried.

Joseph had baby turtles once, and he kept putting them down my blouse, down my back. Blackie took the turtles and flushed them down the toilet. Joseph cried and cried.

Both my parents were animal lovers. Blackie adored their dog, Skippy, but Frances suffered from Asthma. She tolerated the dog and stuck her head out the window now and then to breathe better. How the sooty air helped her asthma, I'll never know.

In his later years, Blackie fed the birds from the fire escape and gave scraps to a stray dog whom he named Rags for the dog's disheveled appearance. He couldn't bring Rags home (no dogs allowed in that apartment), but he was delighted to see Rags one day, looking spiffy, walking on a fancy leash with a kind man that took the dog in. Happy ending.

CHAPTER THREE
THE THREE LITTLE BASTARDS

My mother wanted children. This caused a rift between her and my father. He never wanted any—he told me as much.

"Your mother was a wild woman, game for anything. Danced all night, so much fun, loved the motorcycle, laughed all the time. Then, she wanted to be a mother and ruined everything. Not that I don't love you, but I didn't want kids."

Over the years, my mother became jaundiced about motherhood. Maybe she should have listened to him and skipped that portion of her life's program. When I told her I wanted to have a child, she told me to raise pigs instead because at least you could roast them and eat the meat. (I don't eat pork!)

And, she added, "Remember, they will be *your* kids. Their father won't give a damn, probably leave you, and you'll be stuck with them."

Not very heartwarming or encouraging. But, my brothers and I, somewhere, in our half-orphaned hearts, believed that she loved us and did her best.

When Frances and Giuseppe De Simone moved in to their cold water flat on New Utrecht Avenue between 80th and 81st Street (one of the seedy streets in Bensonhurst), they went from living in the shadow of the El to directly in the darkness under it. (I think they lived with Aunt Phylly until I was born.) They went on to produce, as identified by the hypocritical priest, 3 bastards, Richard, Joanne, and Joseph—my 2 brothers and me. Or, as my mother called us...3 little bastards. Richard was born on the actual D-Day, June 6, 1944, weighing in at 6 pounds, 6 ounces, at 6:00 in the morning. We always wondered if he was the Antichrist.

Frances had 2 miscarriages in the early 1940s, both girls. My mother, though not an overly sentimental person to say the least, always thought it was barbaric that hospitals put a woman who miscarried in the same room with one that had an abundance of flowers and smiling family members, all going gaga over her new baby (even a baby that looked like Edward G. Robinson). She told me it was horrible to leave the hospital "empty-handed." In the years to come, my mother would become an almost empty-handed grandmother, her grandchildren scattered all over the country. But that's another story.

To assuage her grief at these losses, my father brought her a puppy. He asked her to reach into his coat pocket, and she giggled with joy at her new "baby." Skippy was what was called, in those days, a police dog, probably a German shepherd mix. She loved that dog. Skippy lived a charmed life. After Richard was born, Skippy lived his remaining years with the shoemaker down the block. Frances spent time with him every day. Walked him. Pampered him. It was just that Skippy didn't take too well to the new baby in the house.

THE FIRST BASTARD

When Frances became pregnant in 1943, the

doctor told her to stay in bed for the full term, but she concluded that if God wanted her to have the baby, she would be able to fall from Mount Everest. So, she followed her regular daily routine, and all went well. Richard Caesar was a gorgeous blonde, a perfect baby.

His godparents were Aunt Josie and Uncle Caesar (the middle name was always taken from the godparent), who were my parents' maid of honor and best man. The Italian tradition is to name the first boy after the father's father. My mother was not going to be coerced into naming her son Domenico or even the anglicized Dominick. She liked the name Richard, and, as they say, that was that. Richard was always Richard...never shortened. A woman had the nerve to call him Dicky, and Frances nearly threw her in front of a moving car.

There were already 5 boys between my mother's sisters, but Richard was treated like a little prince. According to family recollections, he was an angel. He could have even been the Second Coming. He never gave Frances a moment's woe. Slept through the night from the start. Actually, Richard can sleep through anything. And, he ate anything she put in front of him. Still does. He was extremely fastidious—washed his hands all the time—but wasn't above eating food that dropped on the floor.

As a baby and toddler, he was basically a lump. He was gorgeous, yes. Obedient? Absolutely. However, he didn't walk or talk until he was past his 3rd birthday. But, he made up for it. Richard skipped 2 grades in school and has a mind at genius level. As an adult, he is able to finish the *New York Times* crossword...in ink!

He wasn't athletic—not unless you consider bowling a sport. In that, he excelled. In the bowling alley where he worked at night as a pin-spotter, he was known as Thunder Bay Fats (though he was not fat...it was a take on Minnesota Fats from the film *The*

Hustler.) I always thought he could have gone pro. But, life rolls us up unexpected alleys, and not all of them are strikes, let alone a perfect game.

Richard used to go the movies and stay all day. By himself. At 5 years old. There was the Hollywood Theater on 78th Street and New Utrecht Avenue in those days— later turned into the catering hall, Hollywood Terrace. Frances gave him a quarter, and he had enough for admission and candy. Richard reminded me recently that when he was about 8 years old, he would go to the movies with a little girl, Eileen Volpe. He paid 12 cents admission, 6 cents for a candy bar, and had change left over. The matrons would bring the candy to their seats. These women, dressed in white, looked out for the kids, and, armed with a flashlight, maintained order. No one wanted to piss off the matron! She'd practically carry out the troublemakers.

Three days after Richard's 19th birthday, a man showed up at our apartment. He walked up the stairs, trying to hold his breath to avoid the persistent foul odor in the hallway and call out my brother's name at the same time. The man was from the *Reader's Digest*, and my brother had entered their sweepstakes. He won. First prize.

At first, Richard thought it was a joke, one of his friends from the bowling alley. He had a choice of a brand new car or a brand new boat. Our bathtub was as big as a boat, and there was not much use for a boat under the El, so he chose the car, a 1963 Plymouth Valiant—black with red seats and push button gears. There are more photos of that car than the whole family put together. There's even a shot of Frances leaning into the front seat, with her derrière in full prominence. Imagine a 19-year-old kid from our neighborhood winning a brand new snappy car! We couldn't even afford a tricycle.

While the man from *Reader's Digest* was trying to be kind by not tisk-tisking our home, Richard was in the bathroom vomiting.

"You get to pick out the color."

Baarrff!

"Just go down to the showroom."

Baarrff!

By the time the *Digest* man left, Richard had puked 11 times. I'm sure the man wanted to puke, too. Soon after that big win, Richard put a dime on Number 19 at a local street feast and won a brand new bike for Joseph.

THE MIDDLE BASTARD

I came into the world on Blackie's birthday, December 1, 1948, or so it has been said. His birthday could have been November 30, but Blackie said that he was born a little past midnight on December 1, and I'll stick with that!

Although his name was Giuseppe, the cab-driving, horse-betting, and card-playing world called him Blackie. It was my uncle Rico who alone called him Mandrake the Magician. No one ever called him Joseph or Joe, except for one of his *putanas*, as Frances called them.

My mother wanted to name me Linda Louise. Thank God she abandoned the idea. Though I never liked my name, I can't imagine myself as Linda Louise. She hated the name Josephine, so she kept the "Jo" and added the "anne." In fact, it wasn't her idea at all. My godparents were Aunt Phylly and Uncle Rico, on my mother's side, and Uncle Rico named me. Seems that he kept nudging my mother to name me after my father.

My mother, as the story goes, handed him the birth form before she left the hospital and told him, "Oh, just name her whatever you want."

And, so, here is Joanne Filomena. Maybe it's me, but I thought of names for my children before I had my first period. (When she was young, Frances probably had other things on her mind.) I never had any kids, but I thought about names. I had a doll named Melanie.

I think Richard liked me, for a while, anyway. When I was a baby, my brother stood guard beside my crib with his toy rifle. There was a photo of this, but it was lost over the years.

I didn't like my name until 1958, when Joanne Woodward won an Academy Award for Best Actress for *The Three Faces of Eve*. Same name, same spelling, won an Oscar. All of a sudden, my name was not so bad.

THE LAST BASTARD AND SO ON

Joseph arrived as the big surprise on July 24, 1952. We were all born in leap years, and I found that interesting. Maybe my father "leaped" on my mother every four years. Frances went to see the doctor late in 1951, complaining of fatigue and having missed her period. She told the doctor she was sure that she was experiencing early menopause (at 34), and the doctor assured her that she was experiencing early pregnancy.

Frances actually shouted, "How the hell did this happen?"

She went on to lament that she had a sick mother, a philandering gambler for a husband, and 2 kids already—where would she put this baby? The doctor told her to throw out a dresser and put a crib in its place. And, so she did...after a couple of weeks of shock and denial, followed by calm resignation.

It was a particularly hot summer, as the story goes,

and Frances was past her due date. She was sweeping the sidewalk when Blackie came down the steps with a bucket of cold water and doused her, and labor pains began.

Joseph Americo did not look like Richard or me. We were blonde, blue-eyed. Joseph was black-haired with black eyes. Aunt Louise called him by either Olive Eyes or Butterball. Joseph's godparents were Aunt Louise (Aunt Phylly stepped in as proxy, as Louise had already moved to Missouri) and Uncle Rico.

Planned or unplanned, there he was...the 3rd and final little bastard. Grandma Emelia adored him. Spoiled him. My mother wasn't even able to discipline him. At the first tear that rolled out of his olive eye, Grandma would admonish Frances.

"*Lasciolo!*" (Leave him alone!)

Joseph was 5 when Grandma died. He doesn't remember how much he was loved by her. Believe me, he needed it. In our house, love was scarce. Richard and I taught Joseph to walk when he was about a year old. That was probably the last time we actually touched one another—just enough to keep Joseph from falling.

Where Richard would blow the ants off a sandwich and eat it, Joseph, like me, was fussy. Well, I ate bread and more bread. Joseph ate nothing. He loved milk— that's what sustained him. My mother tried to get him to eat, but he was a mule. Finally, she threw in the towel.

"He'll eat when he's hungry! I'm not going to drive myself crazy."

With me, she tried everything. I hated eggs. She'd put a raw egg in chocolate milk, stir, and try to convince me that the yellow floating around was just chocolate. I used to throw it down the bathroom sink when she wasn't looking. My brothers would make a small hole in the egg and suck on it. Sickening.

Frances forced a tonic down my throat when I was

8 after receiving a note from the teacher: *You should feed this child.* She was mortified. The result was that Joe remained skinny, entering the U.S. Army with a 28-inch waist, while I boasted a bloated 30-inch waist in the fourth grade! Struggled ever since.

To demonstrate my lack of willpower at the sight of a chocolate bar, I tell here what happened at Grandma Emilia's house on 78th Street. I was 5, and Cousin Anthony was about 7. We were rolling a ball back and forth on the kitchen floor. My mother came in and noticed that I had chocolate all over my face.

"What is that, Joanne?" My mother left the room, came back in a flash, scooped me up, and yelled, "Rico, get the car!"

Turned out that the only chocolate Grandma had in the house was X-Lax, and I ate all 16 pieces. Without a stomach pump, I would have exploded in less than an hour. All I remember between then and the hospital is waking up to a Black woman who must have been the nurse holding my hand and saying comforting things. I thought she was an angel, all dressed in white, with her beautiful smiling face.

In addition to being fussy, Joseph had a slight chip on his shoulder. Where Richard and I obeyed Frances, Joseph, when disciplined (after Grandma's passing, of course), would answer back with things like, "When you play you pay!" or, "I didn't ask to be born!"

Ironically, everywhere my mother took Joseph, relatives, friends, and acquaintances marveled at what an angel he was.

I even heard him whisper into my mother's ear, "Excuse me, Mommy, can I use the bathroom here?"

He never mouthed off anywhere but home. Richard and I were aghast that Joseph had the nerve to talk like that. I got smacked for saying the word "punk." (Both brothers behaved in school...not me. I talked too much, resulting in a C in conduct when my brothers brought home A's.)

Little brother Joseph, when he was about 10, was one of those kids that went to the Fresh Air Fund, the one that Eddie Murphy spoke of, where they take kids from the city and bring them out to the country (somewhere on Long Island) for a spell in the open air. Frances was not a fragile woman, but for some reason, she wouldn't rest and smoked like a chimney until she found someone to drive her out there to see if he was all right. We could only see through a fence and tried to find Joseph in the throng of little boys.

When she shouted, "There he is! There he is! Thank God. Let's go home. He's fine!" the relief on her face was palpable.

Did she really see him? Who knows?

When he was 12, Joseph got on a Greyhound bus to visit Aunt Louise and Uncle Rico in Kansas City. I thought that was so brave. My mother smoked about 5 packs of cigarettes until he arrived safely in Missouri. He called from Chicago (reversed the charges), but she still smoked.

Joseph was, and still is, more sports oriented. He played street hockey, in roller skates, well into his 50s. He was known as Hockey Joe Young. Now he's content to watch the games on television.

He won the lottery once...the draft lottery. He came in at number 4, which, in any sport, meant he'd "run out of the money." (I wanted to be drafted and actually regretted not going into the service. I think it's good for everyone.)

After Joseph was drafted and stationed at Fort Dix, New Jersey, we visited him at the base. My father was there for this. He got hold of a car, and we trooped out to see Joseph. Frances was certain that they didn't feed him, so she brought a pot of sauce (gravy) with meatballs, sausage, and *braciole*, along with a big pot to boil the pasta on the barbeque pit. And...the Italian bread. The other visitors stared at us like we came from another planet.

We ate, but Joseph, made even leaner by the military training, hardly touched a bite. My mother noticed that he had mellowed. Maybe the drill sergeant knocked the chip off, for a while anyway. But, he did get lucky in basic training. The drill instructor asked if anyone knew how to type. Joseph raised his hand and spent his Vietnam War time at Fort Sill, Oklahoma, as a Company Clerk...à la *M*A*S*H's* character, Radar!

When Joseph was about a year old, Uncle Arthur took us all for ice cream—me, my mother, Joseph, and Uncle Rico. The car was a 1930-something. When we got home, Frances noticed that she forgot to take Joseph out of the back seat. She called out, but before Uncle Arthur replied, there was Joseph, lying in the street like a turned over cockroach.

Frances just turned to Rico and said, "Would you go get that kid?"

When Joseph was back in my mother's arms, she checked his head and body for bruises. Having found none, she handed Joseph over to Rico and fainted dead away.

Here is where I must include this exchange between Joseph and me when he was about 14. I was dating someone and wanted to get rid of the little brother, as it were. I gave him a quarter and told him to get lost.

He looked at me with his gigantic, sad-looking olive eyes and said, "You know, Joanne, I love you so much, and you don't even like me."

After that, I invited him everywhere.

In contrast, Richard and I never had an affectionate relationship, unless it was to laugh at *Mad* magazine or play word games. As I said, we actually never touched, let alone hugged. We did watch *Days of Our Lives* together for a time, when I came home from school and before he went to work. In one episode, a woman finds out that she is engaged to her long-lost brother. Richard and I looked at each other in disgust.

He said, "I think I'll go in the corner and throw up."

I felt the same way.

We had the same sense of humor, but it wasn't funny when he saw me walking home from school during a hurricane and refused to give me a ride in his new car. Thank God I had the weight to keep me from flying off.

In fact, on windy days, my mother used to yell out the window to Joseph, "Hold on to your sister so you won't blow away."

There was a TV show called *My Mother the Car*. I guess I was My Sister the Anchor!

Frances told me that her 3 little bastards were delivered in different ways. For Richard, Frances was put out with full anesthesia. That gave her nausea. For me, she had a spinal injection that gave her headaches. The doctor assured my mother that if she had a natural birth with Joseph, she'd thank him.

During labor, she cursed the doctor for being born himself. But, when it was over, she did, indeed, thank him. No aftereffects. As long as you call having 3 children in a cold water flat, constantly bumping into furniture, and taking care of an invalid mother with no help from your husband, having no aftereffects. Frances was always proud to say that with each pregnancy, she only gained 11 to 15 pounds, and her figure was restored immediately. I've never had kids, but I'm still trying to restore my figure. Go figure.

Richard began learning the piano at 4 years old, at one dollar a lesson—fairly affordable for any parent, unless one of the parents gambled away his paycheck on a regular basis. But, my mother found the money, somehow. He also took lessons from Mr. Giannelli and practiced at home on a cardboard piano at the table. By the age of 5, he was able to play the *William Tell Overture* and dazzle us with Christmas favorites. By the time the upright pianola arrived, he was on his way to becoming the next Peter Duchin. Sadly, Richard lost interest. But, there are phonograph records (somewhere) with Richard's piano playing.

On one of them, you can hear me, at a year old, pushing him off the piano bench and whining, "Get off there!"

I asked my mother once how Richard was such a gorgeous baby and I was so ugly. She didn't skip a beat.

"Not only were you ugly, you didn't crack a smile until you were 5, and you were always such a crab."

If anyone looks at photos of me as a child, you won't find a smile.

Some time in the early 60s, there was an ad in the paper from Macy's: PIANO SALE, $4.95. Frances insisted that, though it was an apparent typo, Macy's had to honor the price. She put on the girdle, the dress, the hat, and the lipstick, and with the ad securely in her hand went downtown to Fulton Street to claim her 5-dollar piano. Before she and Richard (I later found out that Joseph went with them) left, she found a note from Joseph on the table: *BUY TWO PIANOS, ONE FOR JOANNE.* We couldn't fit a piano bench in the apartment, let alone 2 uprights.

When they arrived at Macy's door, they were met with, "Sorry, folks."

Joseph told me recently that of the hundred people that showed up, Macy's honored about 40. I don't know. I just know that we didn't get one, let alone 2!

When I was about 5 or 6, I voiced my desire to play, but when I told the piano teacher that I didn't like practicing scales and wanted to play "Rhapsody In Blue," Frances shrugged and took me to Miss Barbara's Dance Academy. I liked the idea of looking like Ruby Keeler (perhaps not dancing like her, because she really couldn't dance). I begged my mother to buy me a catchy ensemble—red crinoline skirt, shiny satin polka dot blouse, and black patent leather shoes with huge ribbons, all to wear on my first day at Miss Barbara's.

Lots of little girls were there, lining up for their first tap dancing lesson. I started walking across the wooden floor, which appeared 4 times larger because of the surrounding mirrors, taking my first step to stardom... tap, tap... "We're in the money..." tap, tap... "We got a lot of what it takes to get along..." tap, tap...

Then, I heard a SNAP! The elastic quit on my underwear, and the dingy, worn-out white panties that were washed in lye soap on a scrub board plummeted to my ankles, shrouding my brand new black patent tap shoes and muffling, forever, the sound of my Broadway career.

It's not like we didn't have any fun in the cold water flat. We had lots of made-up games.

For example, right after eating supper, Richard would announce, "Everybody hide on Joseph!"

My nickname should have been Stupid, because I fell for this crap every night! I'd hide in the closet while my brothers locked me in. It wasn't until I stopped screaming and they thought I'd died that they'd open the door.

My mother would just raise her voice a little. "Why do you torment your sister like that?" Shrug.

On the subject of torment, we 3 little bastards would sit at the table and bang our forks and knives to the chant, "We want food! We want food!"

If Frances didn't have her hands full preparing a meal, we got a shoe or a wooden spoon thrown at our heads. Frances was a regular Whitey Ford with footwear and household utensils.

I don't remember why Richard and I called our mother Noodles. However, I do remember Frances walking the pot of beef stew (I still have that pot) from the stove to the table, and her tripping on a loose piece of linoleum—down went the stew, all over the floor. Keep in mind that the floor in the flat was coated in soot and excrement from bugs and mice. But, that didn't stop Richard.

He cried, "Oh, no!" dropped to the floor, and gobbled up the stew. He even sopped up the gravy with Italian bread.

Joseph and I looked on this spectacle with nauseated horror. None of us asked if Frances was hurt in the fall.

There was also the game of flipping bobby pins at one another. We'd fold the little hairclips back, push down on the ends, and then let them fly. One day, my mother found dozens of folded bobby pins all over the apartment.

"Don't do this. You'll put an eye out!"

We also played the charming game of Let's Strangle the Sister. My brothers would take a metal hanger and put it around my neck, and the Brothers Executioners would squeeze both ends until my neck turned purple. Also for fun, Richard liked punching my arm, just to see it turn from pink to green to black. It's amazing I lived so long.

Richard and I made up a game, which we called Tell Eleanor. No one, and I mean no one, but us would understand this game. The answer to saying "Tell Eleanor" was William Powell. Get it? Of course not. "Tell" as in William and "Eleanor" as in Powell equaled William Powell. Can you guess the answer to Crawford Tony? Give up? Joan Bennett. I guess you had to be there.

One Christmas, Joseph was given a toy called Moon Base. It was an "assembly required" kind of thing that when finished would look like the moon surface and an astronaut landing. It was a mess. There were so many little bags filled with pieces and instructions, it was maddening. By the time it actually began looking like the photo on the box, half the room was covered in craters.

Since then, any time Richard and I buy anything that needs to be put together, we yell, "Oh, no! Moon Base!"

I started working at age 10, babysitting for the neighbors' kids—5-year-old twins named Sharon and Karen—for an entire summer for 5 dollars a week. Frances told me that I should have asked for 10.

When I was 16, I got a job at DiCamillo's hardware store on 17th Avenue. I learned how to mix paint and install light fixtures, came to know every nut and bolt in the store, and even delivered horse manure—all for a dollar an hour, 20 hours a week. That was a lot of money!

My brothers teased the hell out of me. They'd knock on the table.

"Who is it?"

"Hardware!"

They thought it was hilarious that a girl worked in a hardware store.

It wasn't funny when my father showed up at the store and said, "Joanne, you don't work here anymore."

Since I had been going to work straight from school, I was always wearing a dress. When the men who were coming into the store invariably asked for something from the top shelves, I'd have to climb the ladder to retrieve the item, and they (I didn't realize this) would look up my skirt. Somehow, the guys who hung around Kelly's Garage—the local mechanic's place situated diagonally across from the hardware store, where everyone got their car fixed—were talking about "the girl who worked at DiCamillo's" and the free show she gave from the top of the ladder. It got back to Blackie.

My career as a hardware attendant ended abruptly with Blackie's declarative sentence. I didn't understand, but I walked out of the store.

When I asked my father, "Why?" he just said, "It's no place for a girl."

One of the older kids on the block told me the reason. I didn't believe him, because I didn't think men actually did those things. In any case, I was out of a job and started babysitting again.

During our years growing up under the El, the 3 little bastards found our own ways to stay sane. Yes, we were a selfish trio, but that was necessary to survive in the coldness of the cold water flat. To be sure, Frances protected us, cared for us, and would take a bullet for any of us, but affection was not her strong suit. And Blackie, a freelance father, charming as he was, did not "fill in the hand," as you'd say in poker.

To fill in those gaps our parents left, we went along, sang songs, played games, and basically dragged ourselves up the best we knew how. No blame. No guilt. As for my thoughts? Well, Blackie warned her, didn't he?

CHAPTER FOUR
IT'S ALL RELATIVE

I always thought it would be wonderful to take a page from *Peggy Sue Got Married* and go back in time to visit with the relatives...

I write here about some members of the family, in no particular order, and with random memories that have stayed with me through the years. In some cases, I've guessed at the facts, or filled in the gaps, or have written what was told to me by others.

Indeed, I have omitted events and truths so as not to openly offend anyone—or perhaps, with some, have my life threatened. Or worse, get sued.

THE TWO GRANDMAS

I've written about my grandmothers in other chapters. I'm sure that the only time Emelia and Francesca were in the same room was at my parents' cheap "football wedding."

Blackie's mother, Francesca, lived with Aunt Millie; Emelia lived with us. I guess there's always one sister who steps up. My mother told me that Blackie would never be homeless because he gave his permission for her mother to live with us.

The two grandmas, though both Italian, could've come from different planets given the vast difference in their personalities. The one thing they shared was their belief in Christ. The priest from St. Finbar's used to come to our apartment to serve Emelia Holy Communion on Sundays. My mother abstained.

I'm sure Francesca also received the Sacrament, but I don't know how that worked. Emelia couldn't walk, but Francesca was healthy, so I suppose she walked to St. Rosalia's for service. Every day, I think, until her later years. Uncle Mike (her son with Grandpa Frank Mollica) described it this way: "She went to church every morning, put money in the basket, and left extra in the poor box."

When her husband, Domenico, died at age 40 (she was about 36, a young widow), Francesca asked the Monsignor for 5 dollars to pay the rent. The food, she told him, she'd grow herself or trade for by doing odd jobs (with her baby, Aunt Millie, still attached to her tit). He told her to "farm her kids out," which is what she did—all except my father, who actually worked the farm, and sickly Tillie, who needed a special diet of goat's milk.

When a child was farmed out, they weren't sent to Disney World, they were sent to a family to work—hard manual labor, which my mother always thought would have done my father a world of good. Though she didn't get the help she'd requested from the Monsignor, Grandma kept going to church because she "worshiped God, not the men who ran His house." That's what Uncle Mike told me.

MORE FROM UNCLE MIKE

When Grandma Francesca was about to give birth to Millie, she asked Domenico to stay close to the house. Her labor had started, and she wanted him to fetch the midwife when the time came. He nodded, gave her a "yeah, yeah," and left to join his buddies in the back room of the corner candy store for a friendly game of cards.

Grandma, in the final blows of labor, just about ready to have her 6th child, took a butcher knife from her kitchen, hid it under her apron, and marched to the candy store. She greeted everyone there with a pleasant smile, walked to the rear, and stepped behind the curtain that separated the rooms.

When my grandfather saw her, he asked, "What are you doing here? A woman in your condition should be in bed!"

She reprised her polite greeting to the other card players, strolled behind her husband, and, with one hand holding her belly, whipped out the knife and put it to his throat.

"I told you to wait with me at home!"

The guys at the card table told Domenico to go home, because by the look on her face, she'd go after them after getting done with him. Her husband nodded, she put down the knife, and they waltzed out together like honeymooners.

Domenico had a brother named Alberto. When Domenico died, Alberto helped Grandma wheel food home from other farms near Bay Parkway. Alberto's wife started a rumor that they were having an affair. As Uncle Mike put it, the woman said he was "helping her pull more than the wagon!" Grandma went to Alberto's home and told him to leave and not to worry if he heard screaming coming from his wife. What happened next?

Your guess is as good as mine.

Grandma Francesca gave me the crucifix that she kept on her dresser. I still have it and keep it on my dresser, facing my bed. Comforting. She also gave me an embroidery of the Lord's Prayer that she told me she made when she was young. I gave it to my cousin Steven's daughter.

A psychic reader told me, "There was a woman in your family with the initial F that died in her 90s. She was laid out in some kind of robes. She wants you to know that she loved you very much, thought you were beautiful, and watches over you all the time."

When I told the reader who the woman was, the reader added, "You and your grandmother were in a convent together in the 14th or 15th century."

A week after the psychic reading, on December 1, I picked up the photo of my father and me that I kept on the dresser and said, "Hey, Blackie, how about a new frame for this to celebrate our birthday?"

When I took the photo out of the frame, there was Grandma Francesca's picture, one when she was fairly young. Now I have them side by side on the dresser with the crucifix. Tableau complete.

When Grandma F. lived across the hall from us on 66th Street, much later than the days under the El, I sat with her quite often, or she'd walk across the hall and invite me in. She spoke Italian (Calabrese dialect), and I understood most of what she said. Grandma used to put raw potatoes on her forehead and wrap a kerchief or rag tightly around as a cure for headaches.

One day, she called me in. She was holding a large box. In it was a peignoir set, a satin and tulle floor-length nightgown and matching overlay, the kind worn by brides on their wedding night. She told me that one of my cousins gave it to her for her 90th birthday, and she giggled at the idea. She was grateful, she told me, but the frills were not for her, and she asked if I would like to have it. I declined. I'm the flannel type, myself. For her birthday, I gave her 5 pounds of potatoes. She loved it.

I remember her eyes, and how she would take my hand in both her gnarled, life-worn hands, and how she'd look at me, and her eyes would sparkle (even through the cataracts). It was an honor to be her granddaughter. I wish my mother hadn't kept her grudge and allowed us more time with Grandma Francesca when we were kids, but I'm still grateful for the short time we shared.

I'll always remember her deep-set eyes, high cheekbones, and silent gait. Never heard her coming. My brother Joseph walks like that. I've been told my eyes have the same shape as hers, but that's where the resemblance ends.

THE CASE OF THE MISSING MADONNA

Grandma Francesca gave my mother a 2-foot statue of the Blessed Mother and told her to light a candle next to it every night. And, so, Frances did, without fail, every night. She kept it on her dresser, and the candlelight flickered until the day she died. When Frances died, I was told by a De Simone family member (by marriage, just like my mother) that the statue had to be kept in the family, not kept by an outsider. I made the case that I was, indeed, a De Simone, and that should count in my favor.

After some back and forth and others getting involved, I left the statue on the living room floor after I cleaned out the apartment, which was still reeking of smoke from the fire 3 months prior. To this day, I don't know what happened to the Madonna. I asked my cousins, but they had no idea. I hope Our Lady found a good home.

Grandma Emelia, the one who lived with us on New Utrecht Avenue, had to be carried everywhere, even to the bathroom. There were no home health aides then. The family was the aide, and, in this case, as with Grandma Francesca, the aide was a daughter.

Incidentally, both Aunt Millie and my mother were born under the sign of Taurus the Bull. Both strong women. Grandma Emelia spoke only Italian (Napolitan) as well. She communicated with the 3 little bastards very little, except for the tsunami of love she had for Joseph. For Richard and me, it was usually, "*Portami il cuscino*" (Bring me the pillow) or, "*Portami un bicchiere d'acqua*" (Bring me a glass of water).

As I wrote in a previous chapter, she did all the food prep, and timed it. My mother was her assistant, really. When the family got together, the other cousins would just say, "Hi, Grandma."

She'd reply, "*Allo, com é stai?*" (Hello, how are you?)

There came a time when my mother was on the verge of collapse. Uncle Rico paid for Grandma's medicine, but my mother carried her most of the time, from her chair to the toilet to the bed. It was exhausting. The doctor told her to get some help, so Aunt Phylly agreed, reluctantly, to take Grandma in for a while.

After 2 days, Grandma begged my mother to take her home. Seemed that Aunt Phylly wasn't the caregiver Frances was, and Grandma, as she put it, felt like a prisoner. Very sad. So, back she came. My mother kept fainting and had to be picked up off the floor many times. Turned out it was her gall bladder, which she didn't tend to for years to come, and it nearly killed her.

I remember Grandma's thick hands, which, unfortunately, both my mother and I inherited. Worker hands—nothing dainty about them. And I remember her bun in the back of her head. Where Grandma

Francesca wore her long tresses in braids, Emilia tied her hair back. Both had black hair, with little gray, well into old age. I inherited that, too.

AUNT TILLIE

One of my father's 2 sisters was given an old-country kind of name; in fact, it is the old country's name—Italia. But, the legacy was forgotten before the ink dried on her birth certificate, and she became known as Tillie.

No one ever knew much about Tillie (except for cousins Michele and Denise, who were close to her—how fortunate for them). She was very private. So much so, that when she was forced to have the obligatory parties at her home—a beautiful place, far beyond the El in the upscale Bay Ridge section of Brooklyn, and more specifically, just off Shore Road, a lush street that overlooks the waters of The Narrows—her guests were escorted directly to the basement for the festivities. Guests were able to get a glimpse of her smartly furnished, roped off living room on the way to the toilet. But, that was as far as most of us got in her home, or in her life.

Aunt Tillie married a wealthy, world-renowned pastry chef and spent the rest of her days behind a bakery counter boxing his cannoli. They had 2 sons, Louis and Robert. I didn't get to know either of them very well.

Aunt Tillie was a sickly child, much like her younger sister, Millie, with no specific ailment, just a weak constitution, susceptible to any germ floating in the air. While most of her siblings were farmed out after the death of her father, no one wanted her.

It was recommended by the neighborhood midwife

that Tillie drink only goat's milk—again, like Millie. This was supposed to build her immune system. At the same time, it provided her with a pet, and my grandmother another mouth to feed, albeit four-legged.

Grandma could not afford to buy a goat, so she bartered. She washed floors and cooked meals for the goat's owner until her labors equaled the weight of the goat, as it was negotiated and calculated. Tillie and the goat stayed at the farm; she took the animal for walks (on a makeshift leash) through the streets of Brooklyn, and her health actually improved. This was also told to me by Uncle Mike.

During one period in their lives, my father and Aunt Tillie did not speak for decades. As the story goes, Blackie asked her for 10,000 dollars—just like that. Ten grand! She refused, citing that he would only gamble it away.

His response? "What the hell do you care what I do with the money? That's my business. You've got plenty."

He didn't get the money.

Every Christmas, Aunt Tillie sent me a pair of stockings, without fail, up until the time I got married. Her husband, Uncle Luigi "Jack" Alba, baked my wedding cake. Everyone at the reception was in awe of it. Really! It had a stairway with a red carpet going up to the top, where the bride and groom stood under a canopy. In fact, the cake was better than the meal.

Every Sunday, we had a big box of pastries, which I thought were delivered. Richard later told me that he used to pick them up (walking from 81st Street to 50th Street). He was able to pass a line of people that snaked around the street, go to the counter, give his name, and the box appeared like magic.

In 2009, Michele, Uncle Mike's daughter, and I had dinner several times at a diner on Long Island. She told me that I reminded her *so much* of Aunt Tillie...the way

I spoke, the way I positioned all the condiments on the table. She said it many times. I asked her if she knew Aunt Tillie's birthday. December 11. A Sagittarius, like me! It still aches that I never got to spend time with her.

My mother held a grudge that Tillie wouldn't give my brother the piano that she was getting rid of, and my father was pissed that he didn't get the gambling money. That meant that none of the 3 little bastards were allowed to talk to her.

I think of Aunt Tillie a lot. I remember her walking on 18th Avenue—tiny, slender, white hair, beautiful smile. How I wanted to walk over to her and ask if she wanted to have a cup of coffee at the Roosevelt Diner. Never did.

AUNT MILLIE

Blackie's other sister, Millie, née Annella and changed to Amelia when she started school, remained the youngest until my widowed grandmother remarried and Uncle Mike came along. Aunt Millie was brimming with style and dignity. The style was her own. The dignity, my mother insisted, was a gift from the Black family that Aunt Millie lived with when Francesca farmed out her children after her husband died. My mother always said that Millie was the best of the lot because of her time with that family, who taught her the true meaning of value and survival. Again, as my mother said, it did her a world of good.

Aunt Millie was a slender, fashionable woman— "clothes horse" was the expression. From head to toe, she was always dressed to the nines in the latest trends. She wore hats with plumes, huge broaches on silk lapels, and gloves. Behind all the fashion and frills was a steely woman with an outrageous sense of humor.

In the family, there was Zia Maria-Rosa (meaning aunt, pronounced "zee"), a stern, wilted woman who lost her husband during WWI and wore black until the day she died, 62 years later. Maria-Rosa visited quite often. Just for shock effect, Aunt Millie answered the door completely naked one day, and she laughed her ass off as the tiny bundle in black buckled on the front stoop. My grandmother thought it was hilarious.

Aunt Millie went to work by subway. One would think that it was a last-minute emergency for her to take the train—perhaps her Rolls-Royce had broken down. That's how glamorous she looked, like a movie star. However, she was not above being outrageous, even on the subway. One day, she was about to take a seat when a man snuck in and sat down. She just sat on his lap, put her arms around his neck, and started chatting as if it was the most natural thing to do. The guy was so embarrassed, he gave her the seat. Everyone on the train applauded.

She worked in a factory, a sweatshop. Even there, she'd do her schtick. At a Christmas party, she showed up disguised in full bag lady costume, including a shopping bag—and, without a word, she filled it with food from the buffet then left the building, leaving everyone staring and whispering, no one wanting to hurt the poor woman's feelings. She came back dressed as herself, and everyone told her about the party crasher. Love it.

Aunt Millie and her friend Marie became weary of being workers. They were both in their 30s, neither had children, and they decided to open a clothing manufacturing factory. According to Uncle Mike, they accomplished their wish with Mob money. They were way ahead of their time. Two women in business and no red light outside. The Family was happy to help 2 ambitious women.

Uncle Mike called Aunt Millie his guardian angel. He told me that she gave him and Aunt Dolly money to buy a home and didn't want to be repaid. Uncle Mike paid it back anyway, but as far as Millie was concerned, it wasn't necessary.

Aunt Millie's husband served in WWII. They got married, and he immediately shipped out and remained out at sea for 3 years. When he sent the telegram that he would be arriving the next day at Grand Central Station, noon, Aunt Millie was there at 6:00 in the morning, stationed on a bench, not moving a muscle.

She told me that she sat next to a woman who kept emoting, waving her arms around, and hugging herself. "My Rocco is coming home! My Rocco is coming home!" When the train arrived and the passengers came through the door, the woman screamed, "Rocco! You're home!" then fainted dead away.

Rocco had to carry his wife to the cabstand.

In contrast, Aunt Millie walked up to her husband and shook his hand. "How are you? Nice to see you."

She told me that for the entire cab ride home, she kept looking at him and wondering, "Who the hell is this guy?"

She said that he was a stranger, having been gone for 3 years. I guess it all worked out.

One night, Aunt Millie was having coffee and cake with my mother and me. Her husband came in and announced that his job had changed. (I have no idea what he was talking about.) Aunt Millie was so delighted at this news that she took off her clothes and danced around the kitchen in her underwear.

One memory stands out crystal clear. It was New Year's Eve in the late 50s. We had all settled in for the night, having been rocked to sleep by the sounds of the train, when all of a sudden, we heard glass shatter. My mother jumped up, ran to a window, looked out, and saw a little group of partiers all dressed in full Native American costumes.

They looked up at my mother, who yelled, "What are you doing here at this time of night?"

She didn't have to ask who was under the clothes—the De Simones are a traveling road show. It was Aunt Millie, Marie, Aunt Josie, and a few others.

All of them, down in the street, just past midnight, started dancing around and calling for my mother, "Come on down, it's early!"

Frances looked over at the broken window, said a few choice words, and added, "Somebody has to pay for that!"

Well, no one did. We had cardboard in that window for months until Frances could scrape up the money to have it replaced.

In the last few years of her life, I was thrilled to spend time with Aunt Millie when she and her husband and Grandma Francesca lived across the hall from us on 66th Street. Millie played a big part in my wedding in 1970 (though Grandma died in June before I got married). She helped with the bridal shower, she fluffed my gown, she checked on me (I had a fever the night before my wedding), and she set up the coffee and cream puffs for the "before" reception at the bride's home.

At the actual reception, she told me that she was so excited, she left the wedding gift at home. It was an honor to know her. She died in 1976, at age 60, of the murderous non-Hodgkin's lymphoma. Sometimes, the good really do die young.

UNCLE JOHN AND AUNT MARY

Everyone called Aunt Mary a saint. She was "good that way." In other words, ask Aunt Mary to do something, and she'd do it, because she was good that way. Aunt Mary was the one that remembered birthdays and anniversaries. She could be called the family genealogist. She had a box of greeting cards for all occasions and never, ever forgot. The cards were signed: *Love, Aunt Mary and Uncle John*, but it was Aunt Mary who remembered. I doubt Uncle John knew his own birthday, which was, I believe, September 3, 1907.

When Aunt Mary and Uncle John visited on Sundays, I could see them from our corner coming down the steps from the El stop 2 blocks away (79th Street on the West End line). They were always dressed for Sunday dinner—Aunt Mary in a dark dress and a hat with a net, very 1950s Mamie Eisenhower, and Uncle John in a snappy suit and tie. Aunt Mary brought 2 cakes in white cardboard boxes tied with candy-cane-colored string. One was always a cheesecake, and the other was a surprise. I was always hoping for a chocolate blackout cake. Sometimes, there was an angel food cake in the other box, which was, sadly, just more cardboard.

Aunt Mary went to church every day to pray for everyone, especially for the soul of her 9-month-old daughter, Emelia, who died of diphtheria in the late 1930s. Aunt Mary prayed but never questioned the will of God. When Aunt Mary died in November 1986 of a quick and painless stroke, there is no doubt she took the express elevator to heaven, where I am certain her little angel, Emelia, was there to welcome her mother.

In their aging years, John and Mary lived in the apartment across the hall at 1783 66th Street, after Grandma Francesca died and Aunt Millie and her husband moved to Dyker Heights. But, Aunt Mary and Uncle John lived for most of their marriage at 388 Myrtle Avenue, Brooklyn, in a railroad apartment. For some reason, it looked so much bigger than ours. The kitchen was large, and seating 10 posed no problem.

My brother Joseph lived with Aunt Mary when my mother was in the hospital for an exploded gall bladder in 1960. He had some really good times there.

There was an El train on Myrtle when we were kids. The ambiance in the neighborhood resembled New Utrecht. Glum. Now, decades later, with the El gone and chi-chi shops and bistros along Myrtle, it has become a hot spot to live and visit. Times do change.

Our cousin Anthony, named for Grandpa, is an electronics genius. Sadly, he's the only male to carry the Ferro name and never had a son. No kids, actually— remained a bachelor. The name died with Antonio Ferro.

Mary and John's daughter, Theresa, was born in 1941, I think. My mother adored her goddaughter. Frances always delighted in how lovely and feminine Theresa was. Slender and tall, blonde and serene, her features were all Ferro. There is no doubt that when my mother had me, she was expecting another Theresa. What a disappointment that must have been!

Theresa married a guy named Joe, and they had a son, Joseph. All evidence points to Theresa having a good life in the Long Island suburbs. She is now a widow with beautiful memories, and a grandchild.

The oldest of my mother's brothers (who lived), Uncle John could barely read or write, but he provided for his family working as a watchman at the Brooklyn Navy Yard. As a child, John had convulsions that left him with a lifelong side effect. When he got nervous, he'd become verbally explosive. Not physically abusive, but loud. All other times, he was as quiet as a church mouse. And, as my mother would say, John was a Dapper Dan and could cut a rug with the best of them. Translation: a nice dresser who can dance.

After Aunt Mary died, Uncle John wandered the streets of his "across the hall" neighborhood (the long stretch of 18th Avenue), where he shoplifted and took home treasures from the trash cans to tinker with broken appliances. He also took up smoking after 40 years. Uncle John was, like his father decades earlier, suffering from dementia. My mother took care of him as best she could, having to go to work to keep a roof over her head. She'd check in on him a few times a day and take him food. He lived alone, and that was not a good thing.

One day when she saw him smoking, Frances went crazy. "He's going to burn the whole goddamn house down."

And, he almost did. In April 1988. It was a nightmare. Uncle John left a cigarette burning on the sofa, and the apartment went up in smoke.

He had to be dragged out as he kept telling the firemen, "Just throw some water on the couch. It's okay."

In the rubble was Aunt Mary and Uncle John's wedding photo, with virtually no damage, atop a charred dresser.

My mother's apartment across the hall landing did not go up in flames but was instead drowned by the fire hoses, clouded in smoke, and left with broken windows. She, too, was dragged out into the street.

But, Frances, always aware of her appearance, told the fireman, "Keep that hose away from my head. I just had my hair done!"

THE SUMMER OF 1988

This segment doesn't belong in this chronicle, but here it is—the worst in my lifetime. Bad enough losing Blackie in '85, then Aunt Mary, and then Uncle John going to a nursing home, having no idea what had happened. Bad enough that my mother's apartment was destroyed, and bad enough that my aunt Tillie, who owned the building, wanted the rent no matter what and dispatched Aunt Josie, my mother's best friend, to collect it. Bad enough that our cousin Steven was diagnosed with cancer, and bad enough that I was married to a prick who had no sympathy for my mother's situation.

All of that was compounded on that fateful night, July 14, 1988, when my then husband and I drove my mother home, having come from his 92-year-old grandmother's wake.

We dropped Frances off, and she said goodnight and started to walk away.

I rolled down my passenger side window and called out to her. "Where do you think you're going without kissing me goodnight?"

She laughed, walked back to the car, held my face in her 2 hands, and kissed it all over. "Happy now?"

I replied that I was very happy and that she should never forget to do that in the future. Turned out there was no future.

By the time my husband and I arrived at our apartment in Queens, the phone was ringing. The neighbor who lived below my mother (who was my aunt Dollie's father) called to tell me that Frances fell and gave him my phone number through the floorboards. The 45-minute ride back to Brooklyn was agony. I knew my mother didn't just fall. Frances would have figured a way to get up!

My gut was telling me what I didn't want to hear. I called the police. I called Aunt Josie, who lived a few blocks away. Aunt Josie called Cousin Arlene. When I arrived, the police had just gotten there, having climbed in from the fire escape because the door was locked. Arlene was there, calling out to my mother. Nothing.

When I saw Frances on the floor, face down,

with one shoe off, I became hysterical. In the kitchen sink was a half-filled glass of water and Frances's last cigarette, apparently dropped before she tried to make it to the door and fell. I sat on the steps that led to the roof, and cried. I was useless.

All I kept hearing was Arlene's voice. "Aunt Frances? Aunt Frances?"

She was taken to the hospital. I called my brother Joseph, but he was at a hockey game. (No cell phones then!) When he showed up, he asked calmly what had happened, and why it took the police over a half-hour to get there, and that we should sue. I was too distraught to think about suing anyone. He was right, though. We should have sued. Perhaps if they had gotten Frances to the hospital sooner, she would have lived past the age of 71.

Next, I called my brother Richard in Arizona. Nothing. In the days before cell phones, good luck reaching anyone unless they actually answered the phone or had an answering machine that weighed 40 pounds. I found his mother-in-law's number and phoned her. She told me that Richard and his wife, Dianna, were somewhere in New Mexico, square dance calling, and that I should not expect him to run to New York for "every little thing."

I stayed calm and told her that she'd better find my brother and tell him to get the hell home! By way of yodeling or donkey dispatch or an armadillo guide, Richard was found. When he called, he wanted to know if coming to New York would upset Frances if she saw him. I told him that Frances was dying, she wouldn't know him, and I needed him. He was on the next plane. That was Monday, July 18.

Frances had had a massive stroke and was lying in the hospital like a head of lettuce in the produce department. Those 4 days were a blur. There was my husband's grandmother's funeral, but I stayed with my mother. I read to her. Stephen King's *Misery*, which I thought was a hilarious dark comedy.

I guess reading any book would have been comical compared to looking at a woman that ran, not walked, everywhere. A woman who worked in a Manhattan office until the day she dropped to the floor. A woman who would wipe the streets with anyone who touched her kids. A woman who buried her philandering, womanizing, habitual gambling husband, and who loved him so much that she followed him to that ugly gravesite in Staten Island in just 2 years and 7 months, to the day, to the hour. Frances died on July 19, 1988 at 8:05 a.m.

On that Tuesday morning, just as Richard and I walked into my Queens apartment after picking him up from LaGuardia Airport, the phone rang.

It was the hospital, informing me, "Your mother is very low."

In hospital terms, that meant that Frances was dead. Sometimes the dark doesn't need an El train. It travels everywhere.

Instead of a one-day viewing like we had for Blackie—who was happy to go and looked great in the box, which was his wish—the torturous wake lasted 3 full days for my mother. I became one of those people that I mocked...the ones that stand next to the coffin as if they can do something to change the fact that her mother is now dead and wearing pink lipstick, a lacquered hairdo, and a beautiful periwinkle blue gown and silver shoes, both which will remain somewhat intact after her mother turns to dust.

They say that when it's needed, we find the strength to do what must be done. Joseph called Amato and Marasco Funeral Home and asked for "the same deal you had for my father." We had a regular wake, my mother on display in that beautiful dress, which I bought because I knew that she would never go anywhere unless she was "dressed." So, why not let her go out in style? The dress cost 200 dollars. When I cleaned out her dresser drawers, I found 200 dollars under her bloomers. That killed me.

So, for 3 days, people poured in, flowers everywhere. I was still numb. Uncle Rico cried openly, but Aunt Josie gently reminded me that, even though I was losing my mother, she was losing her best friend.

Uncle John, who was brought to the wake by Cousin Theresa, sat in the front row and pointed to the casket, telling the other mourners, "That's my sister in there." He also asked Uncle Rico, his brother, if they had met one time at his mother's house.

Cousin Frances (Ronnie's wife at the time), who was dressed in black from head to toe, including fashionable black-framed sunglasses, ran to the coffin holding a wad of wet tissues, screaming, "Aunt Frances! Aunt Frances!" Well, there's always one crier in the bunch.

I didn't cry. Richard didn't cry. After 3 days of this sideshow, just about the time the casket was to be closed, Joseph broke down and sobbed.

It's tradition to have the funeral procession pass the last house where the deceased lived. But, my mother always said that when she died, she wanted the hearse to pass her childhood home on 78th Street, off the El. So, we did. I couldn't help but think about all the money my father won over the years—plenty enough to buy my mother that house...maybe the entire block.

I was always grateful that I was in my late 30s when my parents died, and not one of those little girls whose aunt came to the school to take her home early and had to hear the whispers. "Her father died." How sad I would've felt...

But, on that day, I was angry. The finality of it all. No more Sundays, no more macaroni and meatballs, no more broccoli rabe and beans (though there was one container in the freezer). Our mother was gone. We were leaving Toyland. We were nobody's babies anymore. My brothers and I were now the grownups.

I remember standing at the grave (in a Staten Island cemetery named Oceanview, with no water in sight for miles) when her coffin was ready to descend to her final resting place with her beloved Gi. I looked down and blurted out, "Well, Blackie, you wanted her! Here she is. You better be good to her now!"

It should be noted that Frances, a force to be reckoned with, did not sleep a wink after her Gi died. She kept all the lights on, day and night. She told me that she missed that son of a bitch. He made her laugh. One day, she told me that she saw him standing in the bedroom. I told her that it was a beautiful thing to see her beloved husband.

She yelled, "He's dead! What the hell is he doing in the bedroom?"

Blackie died at 77, on December 19, 1985, at 8:05 a.m. He was diagnosed with lung cancer just a few weeks before and given about a year to live. Blackie was a vain man and did not want to leave this world looking like a withered cancer patient, weighing 50 pounds, bald from chemo treatments. He prayed to die from the moment the doctor gave him the news.

He came home from the hospital to the care of the woman that loved him, unconditionally, for 52 years. He told me, during those final days, that he'd lived more than 3 quarters of a century, lived his life his way, with no regrets, and was happy to leave. While he was in the hospital, he and I blew out 2 candles on a cupcake to mark what would be our last birthday together.

The night before he died, Blackie made a "mess" in

his pajamas and on the floor. My mother cleaned it up, with love.

Blackie was embarrassed, but Frances just looked at him and said, "Gi, we take the good with the bad."

On that same night, Joseph visited and was so shaken by the way Blackie looked that he left and immediately arranged for the funeral, while, as Joseph put it, "I can still think."

During the night, my mother said Blackie called out, "Frances, my chest is on fire. I want you to know that I am praying to God to take me tonight."

When Aunt Mary stopped by in the morning and asked how he was doing, my mother told her that he had a rough night, and she was letting him sleep.

Aunt Mary took a quick look at Blackie. "Frances, he's not sleeping." Mandrake, as Uncle Rico called him, was gone...forever.

Before his passing, Blackie had called me on the phone. "I love you, I love you." His last words to me.

Joseph had arrived earlier to see Blackie "asleep" on the recliner that Blackie hated at first, referring to it as an old man's chair. When I got to the apartment, Frances actually hugged me.

Then she asked, clearly bewildered, "What are we going to do?"

My answer, though it may sound strange at first, brought a smile to her face. "Where do you keep the Hefty bags?"

I was trying to be funny. Blackie would have approved.

My mother just said, "Oh, God!"

You see, Blackie had no life insurance. He believed it would jinx him. When we'd ask what we should do if he died, he'd say, "Put me in a Hefty bag and throw me in the dumpster downstairs in front of the fruit stand."

Of course, the Hefty bag solution was not used.

To pay for the funeral, my mother and my brothers all chipped in. For my portion, I hocked my one-karat emerald cut diamond engagement ring that was given to me by my first husband.

Where to bury Blackie? The guy who didn't believe in buying life insurance always said he wanted to be buried in Green-Wood Cemetery in Brooklyn, where his mother is resting. The cost of a grave in 1985 in Green-Wood was 3,500 dollars. No way. A grave in Oceanview Cemetery on Staten Island (where the garbage dump used to be) sold for 800.

When Frances asked me, "Where will he go?" I said, "Ma, we're going over the Verrazzano!"

All Italians eat after a funeral. Traditionally, the mourners go to a restaurant, like Gargiulo's in Coney Island or Polly-O on New Utrecht Avenue—basically, anything Italian—for lunch after they leave the cemetery. But, after my mother's service, I couldn't swallow a thimble of water. (I actually lost 11 pounds that week.)

Instead of tradition, my husband's mother took charge and put out a spread in her apartment for my family after Frances's funeral. Sandwiches. Very nice, I guess, but I wasn't happy about it. Many friends and relatives declined to join us, so it was mostly immediate family and people from my husband's side that nobody really knew.

I think it would have been better to have all of us, our family, our friends, together, at a restaurant—or even on a park bench eating a Sabrett hot dog (with or without kraut), not afraid to spill the soda—free to celebrate the life of our loved one.

I promise you, I felt my mother's disapproving presence all that day: "They're not family. What the hell are you all doing here?"

The day after my mother's funeral, Uncle Rico

and Cousin Bobby went back to Missouri. They'd been staying with me for the big show, and I was grateful for the company, to cook and care for them, to feel family around me. My put-upon husband went back to work. Richard left earlier that day.

I was alone, sitting on the living room sofa. I picked up the phone to call my mother to tell her all the gossip about the wake and funeral. I picked up that phone for weeks! But, you see, no one was home anymore.

AUNT PHYLLY

Aunt Phylly was my mother's oldest sister—again, the one that lived. Born on April 6, 1910. Her real name was Filomena, legally known as Phyllis, and Phylly to her family. Phylly was tall—5' 6"—considering the height of her 2 sisters that barely made 5'.

She worked at The Metropolitan Life Insurance Company as a clerical supervisor, quite an achievement in the 1960s. To get the job, she told the personnel interviewer that, yes, of course, she had a high school diploma, but the school burned down in 1930, and all the records went up in smoke. Of course, Phyllis had barely any schooling. She was self-taught, and very smart! And, she had a formidable presence. Her wardrobe was fashionable business attire. She had psoriasis on the inside of her wrists and always wore wide bangle bracelets to hide it.

Aunt Phylly had polio when she was a small child and didn't walk again until she was almost 17. As soon as she got back on her feet, she got married. She married a man, a Sicilian, who spent the next 10 years trying to beat her back into the wheelchair. Her decision to divorce Tony, her pugnacious husband, was frowned upon by my grandparents. Whatever happened between a man and his wife was private. Just take your lumps and keep quiet.

Filomena was not the keep quiet type. An Aries. She looked like film actress Mary Astor from the 1930s and 1940s, and she was formidable enough to give movie tough guy Humphrey Bogart a good fight. My mother—who felt fortunate that she had a Calabrese husband that only gambled and slept around—once put a butcher knife to Tony's throat and vowed to kill him if he ever touched her sister again.

Aunt Phylly did get lucky, in a way. She met a man, John, that looked a little like Cary Grant, and she lived the last 20 years of her life, happily, as his mistress. John was a Catholic, married to a woman who was described to us as an "invalid" and who understood that her husband had needs. He adored Aunt Phylly—called her FiFi (a name that stuck when, as a little girl, I tried to say Phylly). His sons also loved and respected her. John cried like a child when his FiFi died on July 18, 1968, at age 58 from pancreatic cancer.

That insidious disease took only 4 months to murder her. The doctors opened her up, saw that there was no hope, and closed her up. She had a stroke on the operating table and lasted one day, struggling to speak, desperately trying to grasp what had happened in the O.R. Aunt Phylly died, moaning, heaving inaudible grunts into the air, clinging violently to Aunt Ruth's hand.

I never really got to know Aunty Phylly, even though she lived only a few doors down from us under the El. She didn't like me, and I never knew why. When I was a child, I loved going to her apartment and spending hours trying on her shoes. She had great shoes. I especially loved a pair of red open-toed "stacked" heels. I inherited her love for shoes and wear the same 7-1/2 size. (My mother wore a 6, Aunt Louise a 5.)

I also used to poke her ninnies and say, "I want big ones like yours!" Well, I got them, and I hate them.

I don't know when the visits ended. What I remember is that her daughter-in-law, Dottie, Nicky's wife, told me (when I was just 9 years old, mind you) that Aunt Phylly was a tramp because she was having an affair with a married man. She told me horror stories about her terrible mother-in-law, who was my mother's sister and my baptism godmother. I guess I was impressed by this somehow—I'm not sure.

What I know is that on the morning Aunt Phylly died, I was at her bedside (I was 19), and she was staring at me, unable to speak but squeezing my hand in some kind of desperation. I couldn't take it. I ran out of the hospital, into the street, and vomited between 2 cars.

I've always been sorry that I didn't get to talk with her more. I wanted to know about the scar on her leg from the operation that helped her walk again, and about how much she loved her father, and how she felt when her 3-day-old daughter, whom she named Emilia, died.

In the months before her death, Aunt Phylly was in agony, and I did some grocery shopping for her. (When I was a kid, she'd let me bring the empty bottles back to the store and keep the refund pennies.) She showed me the X-rays of her stomach area. That's also when she told me how she got the job at the insurance company. Before that, I do not recall having any conversations with her.

I do recall one Christmas when I was about 10 years old, and I bought her a pair of gloves from the glove factory around the corner. They cost 2 dollars. She didn't say thank you to me.

Instead, she turned her attention to my brother Richard, who was also sitting at our dining room table, and said to him, "See, your sister bought me something.

What about you? Shame on you!"

My mother was furious but held her tongue. Aunt Phylly was in charge, and that was that.

Aunt Phylly had 3 sons, Nicky, Anthony (Tony, Jr., also called Junior) and Ronnie (whom she named after the sophisticated Golden Age actor, Ronald Colman.) She got pregnant again after the boys, but in her 8th month, she had a severe gall bladder attack. The operation, back in the late 1930s, was not a simple procedure. They took the baby, whom she named for Grandma, along with the gall bladder. A tragedy.

Aunt Phylly's sons were much older than my brothers and me. By the time I was 8 years old, all 3 of them were already married. We didn't know them when they were kids, but looking at their photos, taken at Grandma and Grandpa's house on 78th Street, you can see their personalities pop off the glossy black-and-white images.

Nicky was a teaser—sometimes a very mean teaser. He always introduced me as his "fat" cousin when I was a kid. (My cousin Paulette told me that he introduced her in that way, too.) I guess he just liked hearing himself say the word. His wife had more than 150 pounds on me, but he called me fat.

He and his wife, Dottie, had a parrot named Alfero. The bird sang "Roll Out the Barrel" on key! It also squawked, "The postman's coming," every time the doorbell rang. Nicky taught it to say "fat bastard" every time Dottie walked in the room. She was always terrified when Nicky would let the bird out to spread its wings and fly around their tiny apartment.

After 9 years of marriage, they had a daughter, Lorraine. Dottie died fairly young, and Nicky lived well into his 80s, having found, from what I understand, a better life in Florida.

Ronnie was a nice enough guy—always seemed

quiet and polite. He was married 3 times. His wife Pat, the one our family knew best, had several miscarriages and a stillborn. After praying to St. Gerard, she gave birth to a baby girl that only lived 3 days. She named her Geraldine, buried her, and went home to an empty, beautifully decorated nursery. She did, eventually, give birth to 2 sons (I think).

Nicky's wife was quick to speculate that they were adopted and that Pat confined herself to her home, presumably under doctor's orders, to pretend she was pregnant. If you ask me, and who's asking...those boys are Pat's and Ronnie's. Period.

After Ronnie and Pat divorced, Ronnie married Frances, the crier at my mother's wake. He married once more, quite happily, and lived a long life with a loving wife. That's always a good ending.

Tony, or Junior, as some of us called him, was the middle son and one of the sweetest guys you'll ever meet. I believe that Tony was born in August 1930. To my mind, he seemed to be the most concerned about his mother. His visits were more regular.

Tony married a beautiful Irish lass named Beatrice. We called her Beatie or Bea. They had 3 daughters, Linda, Patricia, and Donna. When Donna was born, several of the family were at Aunt Phylly's waiting for the news.

The phone call came. "It's a girl!"

If Tony was disappointed that he didn't get the boy the family assumed he might've wanted, after 2 girls, he didn't show it. He smiled and said, "That's good, that's good."

There was a time, a short time, when Tony and Beatie bought a house with Aunt Phylly in a nice, mostly Jewish neighborhood. I don't know what happened, but Aunt Phylly was back in Bensonhurst fairly quickly. Less than a year, I think. Not long after, Tony and Bea divorced. Life takes strange turns. He remarried, and Bea found happiness with a wonderful fellow named Joe.

I have one very vivid memory of Tony. For some reason, when I was about 8 years old, I announced that I was ugly, and Tony asked me, "Who told you that you're ugly?"

I shrugged and said, "Nobody. I just know it."

He quickly replied, "That's not true. You're a very pretty girl, and don't let anyone ever tell you different."

I wasn't convinced, but it was nice to hear.

Italian mothers had a dead aim with any and all utensils and apparel. Frances threw everything at us, whatever she could get her hands on, and Aunt Phylly did the same thing. One day, she hurled a fork at Tony for whatever crime he had committed, when he was a child. It stuck in his forehead. I'm not sure where she was aiming, but the fork bobbed up and down until everyone in the room (including Frances) got over the shock, and Frances finally removed it.

She then spit on her finger, wiped his forehead, and nodded. "He's okay."

That didn't stop them in the future. We all got it in the head at some point, many times.

At the age of 46, Tony died, suddenly. I don't think his daughter Donna ever reconciled his death. She has a good relationship with my brother Joe, who looks like Tony. Perhaps that's comforting to her.

Someone told me, and I'm not sure it's true, but I'll write it here, anyway, that Tony wrote letters to his 3 daughters to be opened upon his death. I'm sure that Linda and Patricia felt his death keenly, but I remember the family talking about young Donna being devastated.

I'll say this, on a more pleasant note. Tony and Beatie made beautiful babies. Linda and Donna resembled their pretty mom, and Patricia's lovely features were more from "our side"—Italian. Although their grandmother Phylly was a stern, in-charge, no-nonsense woman, whenever these 3 little beauties were around, she melted like a stick of butter on hot toast.

Aunt Phylly was the first of the brothers and sisters to die. Her wake and funeral were surreal. While she was laid out at the funeral parlor, Nicky brought a truck to her apartment to take the TV/radio/record player combo console. He'd asked her for it when she was dying, and she told him that he'd never get it, even after she croaked. She kept her word. He brought the lovely furniture piece home, but none of the electronics it housed ever worked. It just sat there, silent. Aunt Phylly was in charge, even in death.

After Phylly died, money was found all over her apartment...under the area rugs, in the sugar bowl, under a lamp base. A treasure hunt without the fun. That's the one thing I kind of inherited from my godmother—an iffy habit of hiding money, "just in case" I need it. Invariably, I forget where I put it, or even that I hid the money at all.

My aunt Ruth, Uncle Rico's wife, who also died too young at age 51, managed to take most of Phylly's clothes and flew back to Kansas City with 2 extra suitcases. I guess that was okay. They wore the same size, and Phylly's clothes were very classy.

I also remember that Dottie demanded that Aunt Phylly's charm bracelet be given to her daughter, Lorraine. After the funeral, Dottie was livid to find the bracelet missing from Aunt Phylly's jewelry box and accused my mother of stealing it. Nobody, I mean nobody, accuses Frances. Yes, Frances took the bracelet—and, as it was told to me, she gave it to Linda, Phylly's first granddaughter, as per Philly's direct order. It was not a request, more like a military command.

Dottie was my Confirmation godmother. She

never passed up an opportunity to belittle me when I was a child and continued the insults into my teens. She told me that I was fat, that I was deformed because my fingers were short and chubby, that I was a pig because I took a second slice of watermelon from the serving plate without asking permission, and that my eyes were too big for my head.

It's still a mystery to me as to why I spent every summer with her and her sisters until I was 11. The first time I spent the summer with her was in 1952, when my mother gave birth to Joseph. I was 3 and a half. (Note here: For my 3rd birthday, I wore a plaid skirt with matching jacket, which can be seen in lots of pictures. I wore the jacket for the next 2 years, in all seasons.)

In 1961, Frances had an exploratory operation for a ruptured gall bladder, and she was in the hospital for over a month. Richard stayed at New Utrecht Ave., Joseph went to Aunt Mary and Uncle John's, and I stayed with Dottie and Nicky. On the evening following the operation, the phone rang at their apartment. Nicky kept nodding and occasionally sighed while he listened.

When he hung up the phone, he announced, "Frances is not going to make it through the night."

I remember my heart sinking. My mother came home, but she was so weak and was unable to speak above a whisper, with a step-ladder incision scar that went from her chest to her groin.

Maybe I kept going to Dottie's because her 5 sisters and her parents, whom I called Grandma and Grandpa, were so wonderful to me. I loved them all, especially the youngest sister, Gloria. She was my idol, someone I wanted to be. Their father played the mandolin in the backyard, and I remember eating bags and bags of pumpkin seeds. The ambiance was so fresh, so green in that yard—so far away from the steel and soot.

It wasn't until I was in my late 20s that I found out that Dottie's family put up with me, and that none of them liked me. Dottie even wrote me a letter when I was about 20, chronicling all my shortcomings.

Before Gloria died of cancer at age 37 or 38, she said to me, "All I can say is that you were very handy to have around, running errands and babysitting."

It was hard to take and shattered the few nice childhood memories I had. More importantly, it made me wary of everyone.

AUNT LOUISE

My favorite aunt, and my mother's other sister, was Aunt Louise (given name, Luisa). What is written about her here is what was told to me by Aunt Phylly, Uncle Rico, my mother, and Louise's son Bobby.

She was born, I believe, on September 23, 1915, and she died on February 7th, 1979. The family always said I resembled her. I'm proud of that. My father described her as "lively." If my father called a woman lively, it was the best compliment he could come up with. She was a natural dark auburn-redhead with bright green eyes, 4' 10", with a tiny figure except for her overgrown bosom.

There is a photo of Aunt Louise looking like Louise Brooks, Hollywood's "it girl," but I think her youngest son Marc has it. When she was a little girl, she was chosen as the billboard model for the Italian liqueur Ferro-China Bisleri, a bitter tasting brew great for stomach ailments.

Aunt Louise started smoking at 10. Her father (Grandpa Antonio) snuck up behind her one day while she sat on a park bench, just as she had taken a Chesterfield out of her pocket.

He whispered in her ear, "Wanna light, little girlie?"

Aunt Louise jumped up and threw the cigarette on the ground. "I wasn't really gonna smoke it, Papa."

Nothing happened. Antonio just laughed.

In her teens, Louise danced the night away at all the local fraternal clubs, and no one at Coney Island swam out in the ocean farther than her. She married at 17 to a balding man named Harry—a Sicilian, to my grandmother's chagrin. She could never understand why her beautiful daughter couldn't find a man who was more like her own husband—tall, blonde, and handsome.

Not to mention Grandma's deep consternation that both Phylly and Louise married Sicilians. In those days, it was a cardinal sin for Italians born on the "boot" to marry a Sicilian. She prayed that Harry didn't live up to the Sicilian man's reputation of having "long hands."

Uncle Harry died in the mid-1960s. It was a tragedy, really. He was stabbed near his heart on New Year's Eve during a home invasion and lasted only 10 months after that.

In 1952, Aunt Louise, Harry, and their 2 teenaged sons, Jimmy and Bobby (Vincent James and Harry Robert, as I recall), moved to Kansas City, Missouri, because the doll-making factory where Harry worked moved its operation to the Midwest. No one knew what went on 1,500 miles away, but in early September 1953, Aunt Louise gave birth to another son, Marc Kenneth. Must have been a cold winter in '52-'53! And, there are no oceans to swim out into in Missouri.

I was only 3 years old when she moved away, but I remember sitting on Grandma's stoop on 78th Street, off New Utrecht Avenue, watching Aunt Louise sitting in the passenger seat of Bobby's white (Buick?) convertible, holding a Philco radio on her lap. As they drove away, I cried and cried. I still hate seeing people I love leave—even to this day.

She loved Harry, to be sure. But, there was no love lost between him and his son Bobby, who said he saw firsthand what his beautiful mother went through (whatever that meant).

Bobby told me once that those Ferro girls are definitely not demure, and they take shit from no one, but that he never understood why Louise never stood up to Harry. Bobby also told me that he and Jimmy were always at Grandma's and Grandpa's house with their cousins but never understood a word their grandparents said. Bobby said that when Harry died, he felt nothing. Sounds like a song from *A Chorus Line*. Sad.

I don't know how Jimmy felt about his home life and childhood. However, my cousin Marc, Aunt Louise's son born in Kansas City, had a loving relationship with his father. I can only imagine that Harry must have mellowed by the time he was born.

When Aunt Louise became pregnant in early 1953, she did not want another baby. She had 2 (absolutely gorgeous!) teenaged sons, and she was done.

Just the year before, Aunt Louise admonished my mother for having Joseph. "What the hell is wrong with you, Frances? You don't need another baby!"

My mother told me that Aunt Louise was given the name of someone who could "help her out" with the unwanted pregnancy. She went to the back entrance of a run down building, through a putrid green windowless corridor, and into a dank room where there was a filthy, bloodstained cot. The "doctor" was a kind of mid-husband, and on a table were his tools. Aunt Louise took one look, turned around, and fled the building as if it was on fire! At that moment, she embraced her pregnancy. It was God's will.

Marc is the family prodigy, and he became a doctor at an age when young men were just finishing college.

Louise never regretted having him, and he became her saving grace after Harry died. Marc took care of her and tried to help her choose a better diet for her diabetes, but Aunt Louise loved her coffee with 3 sugars and a couple of donuts on the side. She died at 64 after going blind and enduring continuous dialysis. Her body was ravaged from the disease, and her former beauty was to be found only in old photographs.

I remember very clearly the morning Aunt Louise telephoned my mother, crying uncontrollably. "I'm blind! Frances, I'm blind!"

It was horrible. She asked my mother to put me on the phone. I couldn't do it. I could not get on the phone. Unbearable! I was crying so much. I still feel terrible that I didn't speak with her that day. My last chance, as it turned out.

There are times I wish I had moved to Kansas City to live with her, but I couldn't leave my mother—even though I knew that life would have been better with Aunt Louise, and I would've been close to my beloved cousin Bobby. When I think of Bobby, my heart melts. We had a special bond. In early pictures of me (wearing something my mother knitted, sewn, or crocheted), there's Bobby!

As I wrote, my heart broke when he drove off with Aunt Louise in 1952. Unlike Jimmy (who I remember being very sweet to me, and as Aunt Annie would say, "Ugh, is that *gorgeous*!") and Marc (equally adorable), who both became educated men, Bobby was blue collar. A firefighter. He had a massive heart attack at 37. Thankfully, Bobby survived and continued to work—not fighting fires, but other well-paying jobs.

Bobby married a woman named Linda, while he was in the Army, sometime in the 1950s. I can describe her in one word. HEAVEN. And, like Aunt Mary, Linda took the express elevator straight to heaven, with no need to be introduced to God. They were old friends.

For some reason, Linda and Bobby divorced. They both remarried and had more kids, but some time in the late 1980s, they were reunited when Bobby visited their kids in Georgia. It was as if the years fell away, and love was in the air and all around!

Bobby had a heart transplant followed by a kidney transplant (donated by his daughter), and the sad irony—which is really what life is all about...irony—was that Bobby died of chicken pox at age 66. It took a while for Linda to follow him, and I'm sure she was okay with leaving this world. They had many happy, loving years together on this earth, and I am sure they are together again.

AUNT JOSIE AND UNCLE ARTHUR

Aunt Josie and my mother were childhood friends. Both women married men from the neighborhood; even closer than that—they married brothers. Aunt Josie married my father's brother Arthur. The circumstances on how Josie married Arthur are somewhat muddled— and perhaps, deliberately so. They lived on the same block. He chased her? It doesn't matter; we'll never get the truth from a De Simone! We were all trained well.

Actually, if truth truly be told, Uncle Arthur was irresistible. I loved him. I don't know how he fared with his own children, but he stepped in when my father was on the lam, and I'll never forget him. I can appreciate the charm of a rogue—not practical, but exciting. He was a bookmaker, a bookie, by trade. The De Simones like to make their own hours. I can still see him sitting at the kitchen table with the racing form (called a scratch sheet), a glass of hot tea, and a fever thermometer, listening to the race results on the radio. An occasional,

"Son of a bitch!" would be heard.

When my 16th birthday rolled around, Blackie was MIA. It was his birthday, too, so it was like half-celebrating. Uncle Arthur came to my little party (pizza from Modica's bakery and soda—black cherry for me) and handed me a 20-dollar bill. He told me it was from my father. It wasn't, I'm sure.

Uncle Arthur taught my brother Richard to drive a car. Richard had a heavy foot. Arthur called him Flounder Foot. When Richard got his license, Uncle Arthur brought around a cruller, meaning a jalopy, or an old car (1940-something) that looked like it was ready to fall apart. It almost did, when Arthur demonstrated to us how sturdy the car was, and instead of kicking the tires, he missed, and his foot went through the metal.

Uncle Arthur told the greatest stories, much like the character Tommy D. in *GoodFellas*—who was, what, there to "amuse you?!" He sat at our kitchen table with a glass of tea and made us laugh. Believe me, in those days, we needed a laugh. He talked, also, about how beautiful his daughters were: BarbaraAnn, or as he said it, BOBRA, and Arlene, his Cookie. BarbaraAnn told me that I am the only one who calls her that—everyone calls her Barbara. We are 6 weeks apart, and since Frances and Josie were close, I always felt that Barbara and I "bonded in the womb."

Her sister is the girly one, 5 years younger. Barbara and I used to get a kick out of Arlene dressing up and primping—adorable. When Arlene was about 5, she came out to the stoop wearing a feather boa and her hair in pin curls. BarbaraAnn and I laughed our heads off when Arlene turned on her heel, draping herself in the boa with a flourish, and retreated into the doorway. A star!

Uncle Arthur told us the following story, but first, it is important to know that the bathroom in their apartment was directly off the kitchen: One day, when Arlene was about 8 or 9, she called out from the bathroom for a towel. Uncle Arthur was sitting at the kitchen table with his usual glass of hot tea, a thermometer, and the racing form, listening to the horse race results. He brought the towel to the bathroom door, and Arlene opened the door a crack, barely enough for the towel to fit through.

"Daddy, turn around, don't look!"

Arthur assured her that he was not looking and went back to the sports news and taking his temperature. Several minutes passed. Then, the bathroom door swung open, and Arlene emerged, naked as a jaybird, and flounced her way into the bedroom.

In addition to his 2 daughters, Uncle Arthur had 2 sons. My cousin Donnie, the oldest son, is a year younger than my brother Richard. If Richard was considered by Frances the Second Coming, then to Josie, Donnie was the Second, Second Coming that came a year and a day later. All Barbara and I heard as kids was, "my Richard" this and, "my Donnie" that. There was no competing with God's son. We just never knew He had 2!

Arthur called his other son, Steven, "The Boy" and added three syllables, A-NA-NA, so Steven became known as The Boy-A-NA-NA. Whatever that meant, we didn't know. But, to this day, every boy that is born in the De Simone family from the Blackie line is known as NA-NA as a tribute to Uncle Arthur, and to Steven, whom my father called Jesse James. So far, we have more than a dozen NA-NA's. Steven, the greatest kid in the world, died much, much too young, but he did leave a NA-NA of his own.

Aunt Josie's entire aura could be summed up in one word: husky. She had a husky body, a husky voice, and a husky laugh. She had a toughness about her, and, frankly, she scared the crap out of me. One "Aaay" from

Aunt Josie sent shivers down my spine.

I always felt safer when she was laughing or singing. Aunt Josie loved to sing. She didn't look exactly like Sophie Tucker, but she sang "Some of These Days" just as convincingly. And she sang it every time she had the opportunity, which was every time there were more than 3 people in the room with her. We loved it!

We used to visit Aunt Josie and my cousins on Saturdays when we were kids. My mother would plop Joseph in the stroller, and Richard and I would walk alongside, holding on to the handle; we'd walk the 13 blocks from 81st Street, under the El, to 67th Street and 15th Avenue, in the shadow of the El.

We would stop at Grandma Francesca's along the way, who lived on the same block. She'd greet us with, "Allo, dollee," her version of, "Hello Dolly," the other English words she knew besides "fug." She also referred to Richard and me as *i figli del sole* (the sunshine children) because we were the only blue-eyed blonde kids in the family. We'd sit at her kitchen table, mute, and wait for my mother to tell us it was time to go.

That was the full sum of our visits to Grandma. (I spent a lot more time with her when she lived across the hall from us on 66th Street.) We never ate a morsel of food at her home; however, Grandma always gave us kids a glass of water. My mother kept her sign-of-the-cross vow from 1935 that she—now we, included—would never eat there again. We did take home some *pasta patane* (macaroni and potatoes) occasionally. Takeout was, apparently, not included in the promise.

I find it singularly regrettable that my mother, stubborn as a mule, kept us from having any part of my father's family, except for Aunt Josie—who, like Frances, was a De Simone by marriage. I'm sure that if she and Josie weren't friends, I would have never known her children. Pity, because there is so much family history there. Rich, funny, and sad stories that the next generations will never know.

There's someone else we'll never know. Blackie told Richard and me (Joseph denies it to this day) that he had a son born in 1934, who, when Blackie spilled the beans in 1984, would've been around 50-ish. Anthony, our other brother, was a retired NYPD police sergeant and had since moved away.

When I asked my mother about it, she fumed. "That whore, Rose, never proved it was his son!" That was all she'd say. Dropped the subject. Period.

Rose? Is that the same Rose whose name I saw permanently inked on my father's arm? The other tattoo is "MOTHER." (My brothers recall that Blackie had only the MOTHER tattoo, so maybe I'm imagining it. I can even picture the red rose!) I always wondered if Frances ever "wiped the streets" with Rose. But, at the risk of repeating myself, nobody gets nothin' from a De Simone—the silence even spills over to the spouses. The Secret Service has nothing on a De Simone!

I think Aunt Josie and Uncle Arthur lived separately, but still married, and remained very close, for some 30 years until Uncle Arthur died in the early 1990s. He's buried with Grandma Francesca and Grandpa Frank at Brooklyn's Green-Wood Cemetery. I wish I could've spent one more hour with him, just to hear him laugh. Aunt Josie died around 2000, and from what I understand, she is also buried at Green-Wood.

In our lives, there was a constant. Aunt Josie did not go into the funeral parlor's room where the departed lay in a coffin. She stayed in the lounge area. We always joked that when Josie passed, she'd be laid out in the lobby so she wouldn't have to go into that room. The best thing to say about Aunt Josie's death is that she left the world before her son Steven. I don't think she would have handled that very well. God can be merciful.

Uncle Arthur had a way of telling the most horrifically sad story, yet making people laugh. When Aunt Millie died, I think she was bald from the chemo and at around 60 pounds. She looked like a shrunken, grotesque caricature of a former beauty queen in a wig. BarbaraAnn, a highly skilled hair stylist and cosmetician, did her best to have Aunt Millie look like... Aunt Millie. Barbara also added a lovely wig. We were all in the lobby lounge when Aunt Josie came in and sat down with us. Here's how it went.

Arthur said, "Josie, Millie doesn't look like herself."

Josie replied, "I understand, Arthur, but this time, I want to go in. I have to see Millie."

Arthur warned, "That's not a good idea."

Josie insisted, "I have to. I can do it."

Arthur said, "All right, I'll go in with you, but listen to me. Stay calm."

When Josie and Arthur came out of the viewing room, Josie left the building as fast as she could. Arthur sat down, calmly, and explained what happened in there. He lit a cigarette and spoke in a hushed tone.

"Didn't I tell her to stay calm? Didn't I tell her not to get excited? Didn't I tell her that Millie doesn't look the same? What does she do? She runs down the aisle, screaming, 'MILLIE! MILLIE!' then throws herself on top of the coffin and tries to hold on to Millie, almost toppling over the casket. Jeez! Then, and I don't know how this happened, but Millie's toupee practically flew off her head! I went up there and pushed Josie back out the room. It's as if I said nothing...like she wasn't even listening." And he continued to smoke, like he was doing an act in a nightclub.

His audience (me, my mother, and a couple of others) was trying to stifle laughs. Everyone thought we were crying. I think Aunt Millie would have enjoyed the laugh, herself.

Seems that funerals bring out the giggles in us. When Grandma Francesca died in June 1970, BarbaraAnn and I walked in that room together. Grandma was a member of the Franciscan Order and was buried in brown robes, not a fancy dress. (She specifically requested that my mother iron the robes for the funeral.) Well, there was Grandma, about 91 years old, looking happy because she knew where she was going—and on the wall was a painting of St. Theresa wearing the same brown robes.

To this day, I don't know what struck Barbara and me, but we had to leave (by the door behind the coffin!) as soon as we saw the painting. We stuffed ourselves into the back room's public telephone booth and struggled to close to door so that no one could hear us almost die laughing. It took many, many attempts to compose ourselves enough to exit through the same door, see Grandma and St. Theresa, and not crack up all over again.

It is noteworthy that Grandma Francesca demanded *no flowers*. But, of course, there's always one relative that doesn't give a damn about what anyone asks for, and so there was one hideous floral arrangement. Between Blackie and Uncle Arthur, there was almost another death that day. I won't say who went against her wishes. It doesn't matter. (Errol Flynn wanted to be cremated and have his ashes tossed in the South Seas. His family stuffed him in a coffin and buried him in Forest Lawn.) Just saying—listen to what people ask for!

UNCLE CAESAR AND AUNT ANNIE

Uncle Caesar (née Silvestri) was my mother's next-to-youngest brother, born October 10, 1919 (?). There was another Caesar before he was born who died at age

2, run over by a truck while he sat on the curb.

Our uncle Caesar was known in Italian as a *pezzo di pane* (piece of bread). It meant that he was a great guy. In Yiddish, he'd be called a *mensch*, a person with integrity. The Yiddish would come in handy after he married a lovely Jewish girl—Ann from the Bronx.

Caesar served in WWII, in Hawaii, for the duration of the war. He was there on that Day of Infamy, December 7, 1941. He was also an amateur boxer—probably could have turned pro. From what I remember of his career, he was a grocery store produce manager.

Uncle Caesar's very own tomato, Aunt Annie, was tall, regal, and sophisticated. (It must have been a shock for her to see the less than demure Ferro sisters curse and yell and cook all that garlic.) They met at a dance hall, maybe The Roseland. Aunt Annie told me that she spotted him, the only non-Jew in the place, and fell in love. She also added that Uncle Caesar was one in a million, meaning that all Italian men are not like him. Their marriage in August 1946 did not go over too well with her family, so they moved in with Grandma and Grandpa Ferro.

When their daughter Helane was born in August 1947, Grandma almost broke out in hives when Aunt Annie refused, respectfully, to baptize the baby in a Catholic Church. Grandma made quite an argument, as I was told. All in Italian, but the message was clear by the number of times she crossed herself in horror.

"*Santa Maria!*" The baby would be in Limbo. The baby would never go to heaven!

Rosary beads were clicking in all the relatives' hands. Saints were summoned. Candles were lit, enough for a wiener roast. The baby *must* be baptized!

Grandpa Antonio was already gone by the time Helane was born, but he would've kept quiet and left the religious matters to his wife. Indeed, out of respect to Grandma, and no thought to the sanctity of the ceremony, Helane was baptized at Our Lady of Guadalupe Catholic Church on 14th Avenue. My mother and Uncle Rico were her godparents.

Soon after, Uncle Caesar, Aunt Annie, and Helane moved to the Bronx (Ogden Avenue?), but they visited all the time. At the same time, all was forgiven in Aunt Annie's family. After all, the baby came from a Jewish mother.

Helane and I were close as kids, always laughing and speaking a butchered Italian. We used to refer to vaginas as *knishes*, easier to say than the Italian slang, *bacsiocola*. That always made us howl.

Whereas I was a skinny kid, Helane was fat—no other word for it. The straps on her shoes cut into her feet. By the time Helane was 13, she was wearing a size 5 dress, and my size 14 was cutting off my oxygen. She grew to be tall, like her mother, with Grandma Emelia's face. A lovely combination. I miss those days with my cousin. I hope she knows that.

One of my most vivid memories, after they moved to the Bronx, was the basket of slippers in all sizes inside the door to their apartment. We all had to take our shoes off and put on a pair of slippers to enter. They had very fashionable furniture, Chinese modern, and the place was immaculate. Same for the other apartment on Castle Hill Avenue, when the girls were older. Aunt Annie always put newspapers on the kitchen floor after she cleaned it, which I think was every hour on the hour. I still don't know what color the floor was.

What did we know about Jewish food? *Nada. Niente. Gornisht.* However, I remember potato *kugel* and *kasha varnishkes*, and I still love those dishes. I do think, however, that Uncle Caesar relished his visits to our dump, where the food reminded him of Mama. He adored pig's feet in gravy—ok, sauce! You would not find pork within a mile of Aunt Annie's kitchen. My mother always made stuffed artichokes and forgot to put them on the table.

A dozen of them would sit on the stove until Uncle Caesar would exclaim, "Frances, you forgot the artichokes!"

If he were a true convert, he would've said, "Oy vey, Frances..."

About 19 years after the baptism-out-of-respect, in the mid-1960s, Helane phoned me to ask if she was ever baptized. She wasn't raised a Catholic and didn't receive Communion or Confirmation, so why now? Helane wanted to marry her Italian-Catholic boyfriend, and the priest needed to know. My mother furnished all the details, and Helane married in a Catholic Church. She went on to receive Confirmation. I was her sponsor.

Helane and her husband brought to the world 2 absolutely beautiful and brilliant girls, Adriann and Dawn. I know they were baptized (I am Dawn's godmother), but I'm not sure they were raised in the Church. I'm not sure that the girls raised their sons in any religion. Times change.

In 1956, Cousin Paulette, Helane's sister, was born. The 9-year gap gave Aunt Annie time to think about religion. She raised Paulette in the Jewish faith. A few years later, Uncle Caesar converted to Judaism and changed his name to Abraham Ferris (if I remember correctly). Seems that when Helane fell for a *goy*, they decided that a house divided was something Aunt Annie couldn't stand.

My mother nearly fell through the floor when she heard that Uncle Caesar converted. When she calmed down, she concluded that no matter his name, no matter his getting circumcised at age 45, no matter his seat in the temple, he was still a wop, with wop blood running through his veins, and no rabbi could ever change that. (Reminds me of the time Richard became a Baptist preacher. My mother shrugged and said, "This is a boy that was not even a good Catholic—now he's a Baptist, whatever that is. Well, it's better than being an alcoholic, I guess.")

Uncle Caesar died of a heart attack in June 1977, much too soon. Today, they would have put a bandage on or a pacemaker in, and he would have lived another 30 years. He'd just gotten his driver's license, and Helane had gotten him a pair of miniature boxing gloves to hang on the car mirror.

Out of respect for our family, Aunt Annie had him laid out in a suit, and not the traditional shroud. She allowed a viewing.

Jews are buried the next day. Very smart. None of that gut-wrenching 3-day circus, staring at a macabre lookalike and enduring the rank smell of dying flowers. Needless to say, our side of the family was shocked to see handsome Uncle Caesar in a plain pine box, without a crucifix watching over him. There were no rosary beads in his hands, no flowers, no screaming cousins dressed in black.

My father walked in, took one look at Uncle Caesar, and walked out. He was sick to his stomach. We were used to the "wardrobe and makeup" send-off with props—satin-lined coffin and a plush pillow for the deceased's head to rest on like he was sleeping (except that the deceased is as stiff as a board, pancaked *punim*, and dressed for the prom). Uncle Caesar looked exactly the way he looked in life. He was not embalmed. He REALLY looked like he was sleeping, which made it all the more strange.

There was no comforting Cousin Paulette, who could have torn the chapel down with her bare hands. She was angry.

"I want my father!"

There was nothing to say. We all just let her let it out. Helane was more reserved, as was Aunt Annie, who kept going to the pine box to kiss Uncle Caesar over and over. It's a night I will never forget.

Uncle Caesar was named after his own Uncle Caesar, who, at age 85, had a massive coronary at the Spring Street subway station and fell onto the tracks, where the train plowed over him. The family was grateful he was dead before he fell. A small blessing.

I'll add Great Aunt Vera here. She was Grandma Emelia's younger sister but much smaller in size. She had 4 daughters (I think). One was named Adeline, who died an old maid, having been in love with Uncle Caesar all her life. Adeline had good taste in men.

Cousin Paulette inherited her father's kindness. If he was "a piece of bread," then Paulette can be called "a good egg." They make a very nice sandwich. Helane moved far from the Bronx and is grandmother to 6 grandsons. Oh, how Uncle Caesar and Aunt Annie would have loved them. She would have worn herself out saying, "Ugh, *gorgeous!*"

UNCLE RICO

Uncle Rico (née Americo) was the last of the 6 living children of Grandma and Grandpa Ferro. Again, the last that lived. He was considered a "change of life" baby, born February 6, 1922, as Grandma Emelia was in her mid-40s when she had him.

Uncle Rico was very smart. He attended Brooklyn Tech High School at a time when the attendees were a select few from each public school. Note that years later, my brother Richard was one of only 4 students in his school (Public School 163, abbreviated PS 163) to be chosen.

Rico was the only one of his siblings to graduate from high school. He never got to use his skills as a furniture designer and maker, but he served in the U.S. Army as a mechanic, where, incidentally, he got his driver's license. The license came in handy because he didn't need all those lovely gray cells to drive a beer truck. His side job was a part-time bookie, supplemental income to care for his mother.

There is a famous story in the family. One night in the early 50s, Uncle Rico was at a high-end poker game with Blackie and some of the other colorfully named gents. Blackie's winnings were up to 50 grand. Fifty grand, sitting on the table in front of him, ready to go in his pocket!

Rico kept telling him to walk away. "Gi, take some of that money home to your wife."

Well, Blackie lost it all that night and had to borrow 10 bucks. I don't think there's anything else to say about it.

Uncle Rico visited Aunt Louise in Kansas City around 1955 and never came back. At age 33, he met the love of his life, Ruth. Since Rico was always a fastidious man, my mother was surprised to learn that his and Ruth's home was somewhat casual—okay, she thought the place was a mess.

He didn't seem to mind, and he made jokes about it. "Ruth, I've been wearing these socks for a week... they're going to walk to the washing machine on their own."

Ruth was what can be described as a dame. Very Jane Russell. I never got to know Ruth, but Joseph visited them in Missouri and stayed for a while when Rico had his heart attack.

Uncle Rico adored Aunt Ruth. He comforted her through 3 miscarriages and a stillborn boy. They gave up the baby thing after that, and Uncle Rico poured all his love into Marc, his nephew. When Rico spoke of Marc, you'd think he gave birth to him. Such love in his eyes!

Aunt Ruth died when she was 51, after suffering from a myriad of illnesses. Rico was devastated. Cried and cried. It was heartbreaking.

A few years later, at my father's wake, he introduced us to Lil, a lovely woman, born in Arkansas, who had retained her southern belle accent. I got to know Aunt Lil very well. Too bad Aunt Louise was already gone. Uncle Rico took me to her grave, and I blinked back tears at seeing her name on the stone.

Visits to Uncle Rico and Aunt Lil's Kansas City home were like spending time at Little House on the Prairie. She wore the eyelet-brimmed cap and ankle-length floral flannel nightgown to bed. How do I know this? She graciously invited me to sleep in her bed, while Uncle Rico slept in the den. I would have been just as happy in the den to let him sleep with Tootsie.

Everything in their home wore a hat—a crocheted cover—from the toaster to the toilet paper. I loved it. Aunt Lil made everything feel warm and cozy, and it was easy to pack on the pounds from her delectable calorie-laden meals.

Early in 1996, I was going to visit them, but a snowstorm in New York grounded all flights. I called Uncle Rico and asked if I could postpone the trip until May, when the weather would be more cooperative.

He paused, a long pause, then replied, "I guess, well, I think that will be okay."

That May visit was my last. Uncle Rico died on July 11. Let me say that we should all die like Uncle Rico. He sat down, closed his eyes, his dentures fell to the floor, and that was that.

UNCLE TONY

I guess you can call Uncle Tony the runt of the litter, and the only one of my father's brothers to go bald. While his brothers had darker names such as Blackie, Arty Black, and Black Mike, he was known as Billyhop. Rumor has it that Tony used to "have his way" with the goat when he was a teen living on the farm. Not sure if his nickname had anything to do with the goat.

Tony was married to Jenny, who was Aunt Millie's husband's sister. Seems that, except for Frances, all the in-laws' families were either directly related or from the same town in Calabria. Jenny and Tony had a daughter, Frances, who used to give me her old clothes when I was a teen. They were gorgeous. For anyone who watched the film *The Help*, Skeeter wore the same orange sheath dress with the short capri jacket in one of the scenes. I loved the outfits Frances gave me. I felt so grown up. I was told that she died fairly young, but I don't know the details.

Tony and Jenny lived near Coney Island, behind the watermelon stands. (In that area, later on, Pathmark supermarket replaced the stands, and those beachy houses were gone.) There were some great parties in that house. They were like vaudeville shows, with skits and songs—all improv. Aunt Millie's trunk (yes, an actual trunk) was filled with costumes, wigs, masks, and props. Whatever mayhem was cooked up by Millie and her friend Marie, along with some of the other featured players, there was always a show. We were all invited to do something. Sometimes I sang. Arlene and Steven did their version of *The Honeymooners*.

One night stands out in my memory. Aunt Millie and Marie were dressed as doctors, the whole getup. One of the men was wheeled in wearing a hospital gown over his clothes. Wheeled in on what? I don't remember—looked like a gurney. He was transferred to the dining room table and began to scream.

The women were chanting, "It's almost here. Hang in there. You're doing great!"

A little while later, the "doctors" reached under the gown and pulled out a doll. Then the whole place erupted into applause, passing the baby around.

That was a typical party. And it should be noted that the De Simones needed no excuse to put on a show. It's in the blood. Don't know where it comes from!

After Aunt Jenny died, Uncle Tony's mission was to have a woman. He was a sexual animal until he died in his mid-80s. I remember noticing Tony at my mother's wake, bragging that he was 82 and flexing his muscles to any mourner who walked in the door. He was quite a character, but then...he was a De Simone, wasn't he?

UNCLE MIKE AND AUNT DOLLY

Grandma Francesca was widowed in 1916 (I think). Aunt Millie was just a baby. Grandma had, as I mentioned, 6 kids. Uncle Mike was a Mollica, the son of her 2nd husband, but with very much a De Simone sense of humor. A great guy!

In 2008, I was so thrilled to see him again when Cousin Michele invited me to her home. I looked at Uncle Mike, and it was like Blackie and Artie both coming back to life. The manner, the voice, the eyes. A few weeks after that wonderful visit, I spent some time with Uncle Mike in the hospital shortly before he died at age 85 or 86.

He told me this story: After Domenico De Simone died, Grandma had it rough. She met Frank Mollica, married him, and had her 7th child, Michele. When they met, Grandpa Frank was in Brooklyn to work and make enough money to send back to Italy, enough for his wife and 5 children to come to America. That plan was shot to hell.

Growing up, my brothers and I never knew that Grandpa was not our biological grandfather. Didn't matter.

When he died, I remember Grandma saying (in Italian), when she saw him laid out, "He never looked better!"

I always wondered where Domenico De Simone was buried.

When Grandma joined Grandpa Frank in Green-Wood Cemetery, and we were all standing around the grave, Aunt Millie whispered to the ground, *"Papa, ho portato la mamma. Non sei più sola."* (Papa, I brought Mama. You're not alone anymore.)

Aunt Dolly (née Filomena) was a lovely woman. I remember her wedding picture, where she was sitting on the floor with her beautiful gown spread out all around, with Uncle Mike behind her, his cheek close to hers. So lovely. So much love. They had a beautiful life together. Their daughters, Michele and Denise, are wonderful girls who took the lesson of their parents' love into their lives. Both are accomplished, happily married women and the pride of any family.

My father's 1st cousin, whom my cousins called Aunt Vera, was strictly called Cousin Vera by my brothers and me. My cousins, out of respect, I'm sure, called a lot of older relatives, and even friends and neighbors, aunt and uncle. But, my mother was a purist. An aunt is an aunt, a cousin is a cousin, and a friend is called by her last name, i.e., Mrs. Balcucci.

Cousin Vera was an adorable kook. She once served her guests a plate of pasta with a poached egg on top, because she believed that a meal needed some protein. She had a lovely figure and the most beautiful skin. Her face was pure natural beauty. To my recollection, Vera died nearing 100.

Some relatives I never met, having died before I was born, or their lives were lived away from our little circle. My 2nd cousin Josephine Ferro lived on 78th Street. We were friendly, but not close. Others we saw at funerals, and some at weddings. Everyone from my parents' generation is gone. Some of my cousins are gone. It's just life doing what life does.

CHAPTER FIVE
FELLAS OF THE CAFÉ ESPRESSO

The Café Espresso existed for a time, on New Utrecht Avenue, between 80th and 81st streets, 2 doors down from where we grew up. It was a hangout for mobsters, the kind of place one can see in a Scorsese movie. The fellas at the Café Espresso were the "good guys" that ruled the neighborhood—there was no need for traditional law enforcement. No one locked their doors. Windows were left open to air out the houses. Robberies did not exist. A thief would have to have had a death wish to even consider stealing.

Some of The Guys gave us quarters whenever they saw us. This happened a few times a week. We always took the money to Freitag's ice cream parlor for a frappe, which cost 25 cents with a side of seltzer. On special occasions, like birthdays and holidays, we got a dollar. Joe Colombo, one of The Guys, gave us money and even small gifts like Italian cookies or licorice sticks. Joe was even more generous at Christmas time.

Once in a while, in the summer, he would drive some of us kids in his swanky convertible Cadillac to a place with horses, trees, open air, and wonderful food. It was such a treat to leave the sweltering heat of the El, even for a day. (The first time we went there, I thought it was a surprise—that he was bringing me back to my real parents, Roy Rogers and Dale Evans. More on this later).

Junior, a small-time hood, lived with his dog named Jammed Up in the poshly renovated apartment beneath the Eterno family and above the Café Espresso. He was an all-around gopher, a janitor of sorts, a card game coordinator, and a watchman. He cried like a baby when the dog died.

The Eterno family, having moved to Brooklyn from Sicily around 1958, had a good rapport with The Guys, who enjoyed being around the kids that spoke only Italian at home. There is much more history of the Eterno family, but for this memoir, I'll only say that while other kids were outside playing every Saturday, the Eterno clan was busy doing household chores. Or, as one of them would say, "We wash the house on Saturday."

As I mentioned, and everyone in the neighborhood knew, the Café Espresso was a front for local racketeering, numbers running, card games in the back room, and who knows what else. The apartment upstairs was the formal dining room and catering hall, with the bedroom in the back for Junior and anyone else who was too tired to go home after an all-night poker game. Before it was renovated, it looked just like ours. When it was done, it looked like a palace, complete with a "Hollywood kitchen," a stocked bar, and plush sofas—amenities found in the houses *around the corner*. If the place was ever used to invite women over, we never saw it happen.

Ralphie Boxcar was another hood not too high up in the ranks, but a pugnacious punk. He sent his 2 sleazy sons and 4 more hoodlum teens to "take care of" my brother Richard for giving a pain-in-the-neck kid from the block a boot in the pants. Those punks beat my brother unconscious and unrecognizable, leaving him for dead in the street. Richard was laid up for days—it was horrible.

Frances went to the Café in a fury and called the goodfella a coward for sending 6 against one. If my mother had had a gun, I have no doubt that she would have taken them all out. Joe Colombo apologized and tried to give Frances a couple of bucks, but she refused. Where was Blackie? Still don't know. We did find out that Joe Colombo "handled it." He liked Blackie and respected my mother's gumption. How he went about handling it, we'll never know.

Aside from the Ouija board debacle (story coming) and the monsters that beat up my brother, it was comforting to see the men in suits hang around. There were always spiffy cars pulling up, and the wonderful aroma of Italian food permeated the sooty air under the El. I think Mr. Eterno did some of the cooking. He was a nice man and a great cook, as I recall.

OUIJA, THE MYSTIC HANDICAPPER

Before I learned to read *See Spot Run*, I was able to handicap horses and see Seabiscuit run. My father, being a cab driver by night but a gambler by trade, taught me to read a scratch sheet before I was able to recognize my own name on paper. He was so proud, you'd think I was a child prodigy of the ancient Hebrew Torah.

At first, when I was 2 or 3, he'd have me close my eyes and point at the racing form, and wherever my finger would land on the sheet, that was the horse he'd bet on. Somewhere in the Bible, it is written, "...and a little child shall lead them..." Well, not so at Aqueduct Racetrack. I never picked a winner. I should have remembered that when I started dating.

However, I did learn about "the flats," where the jockeys sit right on the horse. "Real horse racing," my father called it. The other kind was harness racing, or "the trotters," which were known in our family as "the farmers." No real gambler would waste his money on them.

Blackie schooled me on fillies, mares, the difference between stallions and geldings (another thing I should've remembered when I started dating), last times out, the odds, betting across the board, weather conditions, and the total mutual handle—the total amount of money taken in that day at a certain racetrack. I became a chip off the old block, though just in theory. I placed my one and only bet on a horse when I was 25—a big 2 dollars. I lost, and I realized that some things work out better on paper.

For my 15th birthday, Richard gave me a Ouija board. My friends and I would sit around it, placing our hands on the mystic oracle (the thing that moves around the board), and ask it the usual Doris Day questions. "Will I be pretty?" "Will I be rich?" Que será!

I think this Ouija board was Italian, because it only responded to my friend Marie's inquires, who called the board Luigi. She was particularly adept at getting the piece to move around the board and answer our questions.

"Luigi, are you with me?" she'd ask respectfully.

It would take many years to find out whether or not the predictions were true, because some of the things we wanted to know were about marriage, children, and death.

As I've mentioned before, I come from a family of professional and part-time bookies. My father's brother Artie Black made his living that way, and my mother's brother Rico (a furniture carver turned truck driver when straight-lined furniture came into fashion in the early '50s) moonlighted as a numbers runner to pay for my grandmother's arsenal of medication. At the time, it cost a hefty 85 dollars a month. My mother even helped him out in the late '40s, right after I was born, by taking number orders on the phone. But, she was immediately arrested by 4 police officers who climbed in the window from the fire escape and took her downtown.

She informed them that she was an innocent nursing mother, and should they wake the baby, she'd wipe New Utrecht Avenue with the entire police force. She was released for lack of evidence. This episode took place at Aunt Phylly's, where I think we lived for a short time after I was born. Strange that on that day, Uncle Rico decided to take Aunt Phylly to the movies.

One way to play the numbers was to try to guess what the last 3 numbers of the total mutual handle would be at a certain track on a given day. For instance, if you placed a bet for a dollar on the number 427, and the track took in 1,695,427 dollars, you'd win 500 dollars. You'd see the number in the racing section of the newspaper the next day then call your bookie to collect your winnings. Winners never saw the full 500 dollars because bookies took their cut. But, it was really very simple and not a bad racket for the bookie, since he collected his cut, win or lose.

One day, after school, my kid brother Joseph watched on as I fooled around with the Ouija board.

"Wee-gee, are you with me?"

Nothing.

More determined, "Wee-gee, are you with me?"

Nothing.

Then I decided to use the Marie method. "Luigi, are you with me?"

To my surprise, the mystical Italian oracle shot to the word YES printed on the board.

For laughs, I asked it, "What will the last 3 numbers of the total mutual handle at Hialeah be for February 15, 1965?"

It slowly moved around the board, stopped on the number 3, slid along and rested on number 7, and finally ended on number 9. Joseph's eyes were like saucers.

When my mother came home from work, I told her that the Ouija board said that 379 would be that night's winning number at Hialeah Park Race Track. She called her friend Barbara Bono, a delightful Jewish woman who picked up some Italian phrases from her former husband.

Barbara, impressed by this sign from the betting gods, exclaimed in her Yid-talian, "*Marone*, no kidding! I'll call my bookie, Tony the Baker."

So, the bet was in. One dollar on 379. That night, it was Joseph's turn to go to the candy store to pick up the newspapers. The winning number would be in the *Daily News*. We heard Joseph running up the steps, trying to breathe and talk at the same time.

"Oh, my God!"

We thought somebody died.

He threw open the door and fell on the floor with the open *Daily News* stretched out. "You won, you won! You hit the number!"

I kicked him in the ass.

"Get out of here—you're lying."

With renewed pleas and elevated fervor, he screamed, "Joanne, I swear, look at the paper. You won!"

After several minutes of watching my brother contort, just as he began foaming, I slowly reached for the paper. There it was, the last 3 numbers of the total mutual handle at Hialeah...379! My mouth fell open. My mother tore the paper from my hand. I picked Joseph up from the floor, and we jumped around like 2 itchy monkeys.

The phone rang. It was Barbara Bono. My mother listened, her lips tightened in what we referred to as "the Frances."

She spoke through gritted teeth. "Is that so? Well, we'll just see about that!" She hung up the phone and dialed another number. "Arthur? Frances. My daughter hit the number tonight, but the bookie won't pay up. Says he's not paying no kid. Who? Tony the Baker. Okay, I'll wait."

A few minutes later, the phone rang again. This time, it was Tony the Baker himself.

My mother's jaw loosened. "We'll be there."

The next morning, at 11:00 a.m. sharp, my mother and I went to the meat department of the A&P, where we met with Tony the Baker.

"Why didn't you tell me your uncle was Artie Black? This was a misunderstanding, that's all." He took a wad of bills from his hip pocket. "Hold out your hand, kid."

I looked at my mother.

"Go ahead," she said. "It's your money."

I held out my hand, palm up, and Tony the Baker gently laid 6 crisp 50-dollar bills in it.

Without closing my hand on the money, I moved my hand toward my mother. "Here."

She looked at me with a mixture of pride and disappointment—proud of me for offering the money, and disappointed in herself for needing it. "That's your money. You won it," she said softly.

"No, you take it," I said.

It didn't matter that our jackpot was only 300 dollars. No doubt, everyone from Tony the Baker to Barbara Bono got their cut. But, for us, 300 dollars was a fortune. The following day, my mother bought our very first sofa.

On the same day that my mother was picking out her blue velvet sofa and having it fitted for its custom-made, suffocating plastic cover, dozens of guys in suits were making the pilgrimage to the small triangular block under the El where a 15-year-old kid with a Ouija board was about to make them rich. When I got home after school, I was greeted enthusiastically by men dressed in shiny sharkskin and spit-shined shoes.

These were men who had names like Ralphie Boxcar, Stretch D'Amato, Louie the Lug, Charlie the Juice, and many others, including my new best friend, Tony the Baker.

"Here she is! She's here! Aay, come here, kid. How ya doin'?"

It was a chorus of bookies and players who were smiling, patting my back, shaking my hand, and rubbing my head. "We're here for the number, kid. Yeah, Tony told us about it. You got the number from the Ouija board. That's great."

Ralphie Boxcar put his arm around my shoulder. "Now, kid, we'll all wait here. You go upstairs and ask the Ouija board the number for tonight, ya hear?" He ushered me through my downstairs doorway and to the foot of the stairs.

I smiled and waved, went upstairs, and waited a while, pretending to ask Ouija what the last 3 numbers of the total mutual handle would be for that night. I didn't want to tell those well turned out goons waiting downstairs that my uncle Arty Black paid us a visit at 6:00 a.m. that very morning and woke me up with a bribe—a box of jelly tarts from Siegel's bakery.

"Sweetheart, get out that board thing. Let's see what the number's gonna be today."

I nodded drowsily, got the Ouija board, and placed it on the table.

"Is this the same place you had it yesterday?" he asked, wanting to be sure the vibes would not be shaken or stirred—no room for chance errors.

I answered yes and began with the question, "Luigi, are you with me?"

The little plastic answer man swiftly moved to YES.

"Cheesus, Joanne, you sure you ain't movin' it yourself?"

I shushed him and asked about that day's last 3 numbers of the total mutual handle. The Ouija responded in form...2...1...0.

"The number is 210," I said when the oracle stopped.

Arty Black stayed long enough for a glass of tea and a jelly tart. He left with the smile of a winner that found a new and perfect system to beat the odds. The magical, mystical Ouija guided by Italian angels was gonna put us all on easy street.

My public was waiting downstairs. I strode down like a celebrity and announced, "The number for today is 210."

The men in suits were silent for a moment and then reprised the backslapping, head rubbing, mingling, hand shaking, nodding, and soft shoeing.

That night, the number was 215, and my celebrity came to a halt. I was a one-hit wonder. The clock stopped on my 15 minutes of fame.

When I came home from school the next day, all the guys were gathered in the window of the Café Espresso, two doors down. The same guys that loved me the day before were shaking their fists and cursing in Italian.

Uncle Arthur was so mad. "Throw that thing in the garbage!"

As long as he didn't want the jelly tarts back.

I guess that Ouija, the mystic handicapper, was willing to give my mother a new sofa. The rest of the furniture was up to us.

CHAPTER SIX
NEIGHBORS

The block we lived on was shaped in a sharp triangle, like a slice of pie. There was only one building on the block, a cemented chain of apartments above storefronts and factories, or sweatshops, where immigrant women spoke in Italian and did piecework. The dwellings occupied the 2nd and 3rd stories of each building.

The entire 3-sided structure was connected by a center opening, generously referred to as a courtyard, where the neighbors from under the El and *around the corner* shared clotheslines, gossip, and, sometimes, their secrets. Voices carried.

The courtyard was a dreary place, accessible only via the even more abysmal cellars that housed scary crannies, spiderwebs, and nests of rodents and insects of varied species. Richard and I had Halloween parties down there. We never needed to buy any decorations.

Fire escapes were attached to the buildings on the courtyard side. In the event of fire, we would have to climb down into the courtyard and hope one of the neighbors' cellar doors was left unlocked. I don't recall there ever being a fire, but we all knew the drill.

The only time anyone stepped foot into that

courtyard was to retrieve a garment that fell from the clothesline. And, if you had the unfortunate experience of having to go down there and happened to look up, it was like being in a snake pit.

BIG MOUTH PAULINE

Since the clotheslines were attached to both sides, they had to be shared, and the women had an unwritten hanging schedule. We shared our line with Sally, who washed clothes on Mondays. If it rained, Tuesdays.

Sally had a son named Sonny, a professional ice skater. My mother called him a bachelor. When I asked what a bachelor was, she said it was a man that wasn't married. I told her that I heard someone say Sonny was queer.

"What's queer?" I asked.

"A man that never gets married."

End of inquiry.

Pauline, or Big Mouth, as Frances called her, rarely left her apartment but knew everything about everyone. She had her husband run the household errands after he came home from work, which left Pauline the entire day to cook and clean and listen.

Her voice was piercing, and as soon as she heard the squeak, squeak of the clothesline moving, she'd open her window, stick her head out, locate the sound, and begin, "Did you hear about...?"

One Sunday evening, my mother asked me to go to the store to buy milk.

"Where do I get milk now? Everybody's closed."

Before Frances could say a word, Pauline's voice punctured the courtyard air. "Charlie's open on 82nd!"

One day, she caught Sally's ear. "Did you see what Frances did? She had that colored woman, you know, the Super for the building across the street on New Utrecht? Frances had her up, and the colored woman left with a bag!"

How Pauline could see from around the corner and through the brick remains a mystery.

After my father had been MIA from life under the El, on the lam from the bookies, Pauline had the bad taste to ask my mother why she hadn't seen him around lately.

Frances faced her with a tight lip and her penetrating, cold blue eyes. "He works nights."

Frances spoke with such finality, that even Pauline was speechless.

Pauline always bragged about being the mother of the most beautiful girl on the block—which she was, to some. (I always thought that Francine Dasaro was the winner.) She made it a point to point out that her daughter, Catherine, didn't have to wear hand-me-downs or her brother's sweaters. If this kind of talk angered my mother, I never knew it. I only knew that Frances had no use for Pauline.

Pauline caught me smoking a cigarette when I was about 14. She couldn't wait to tell my mother, and in one of her rare outdoor appearances, she cornered her.

"Frances, do you know that I saw your daughter smoking today?"

My mother smiled. "Thank you, Pauline, but my daughter has my permission to smoke."

Frances kicked my behind real good that day.

I pleaded, "But, you told Pauline I have permission!"

She responded, "I wouldn't give Big Mouth the satisfaction."

It was no secret that Frances disliked Pauline, but when Pauline gossiped to everyone that her neighbor's daughter was knocked up, news she heard first hand through the paper-thin walls, it was my mother's turn to corner Pauline.

"You better keep your mouth shut! We're raising daughters, too. Remember, when you spit in the sky, it can come down to hit you in the eye."

Years later, we heard that Pauline had died from cancer of the mouth.

My mother shook her head. "God scares me sometimes."

KARL AND MARTHA

Karl and Martha lived in the apartment above ours. Martha never used the clothesline, so her line-mate, Carmelina, washed her clothes whenever she wanted. In fact, we were convinced that Martha never washed her clothes or anything else.

There was a persistent foul odor in our hallway, which can only be described as farts boiling in old sock water. When we came in the downstairs front door, we held our breath until we reached our landing and quickly sped inside our apartment.

Karl and Martha were survivors of the Holocaust. On their mailbox were 2 names, Kraus and Deutsch. We didn't know who was who, and my mother said they were married but Martha kept her own last name because it was a common law marriage. Frances never completely evaded a question; instead, her answers were meant to close the subject immediately.

Karl had a number tattooed on his wrist, which we saw in detail when he didn't make it up the 2 flights of stairs and lay on the steps in a drunken stupor, the front of his trousers soaked in urine. He also had 3 fingers missing from his right hand, so that the remaining forefinger and pinky formed an absurd U effect.

Sometimes, he made it home in one piece, but

it was a slow, agonizing, staggering journey from the train station 3 blocks away, with frequent stops to lean on cars or fire hydrants.

When he'd reach the top step of their landing, we could hear Martha's voice bellowing, "Get out! Get out! Get out, you drunken bum, you!"

My brothers and I would laugh. "Martha's at it again!"

Frances would give us all a smack in the back of the head. "Have some respect. That man was in a concentration camp. He was tortured by Nazis. He has the right to drink. You little bastards would drink, too, if you went through what he went through!"

At 5 or 6, I had no idea what a concentration camp was, except that people were put there by Nazis and got tortured and tattooed. When they got out, they earned respect and the right to get drunk.

We never went past our landing. Up those stairs and behind that door were unspeakable horrors: the nasty smells, the battles in a foreign language, the overall gloom. We called it the "inner sanctum."

One day, as I was just about to go into our door, still holding my breath, I heard a familiar gravely voice from above.

"Johanna, Johanna?"

I was frozen with fear. It was Martha. Oh, God, that sounds like she's saying my name!

"Come up 'ere for a minute," Martha said softly in her German accent.

I couldn't speak. I exhaled like someone punched me in the stomach. My legs were like jelly, but I obeyed and forced them to move up the stairs.

Martha was standing at the door of the inner sanctum, waving her hand encouragingly. "Come in, come in."

I entered on wobbly legs, and she closed the door

behind us. The place smelled like a stale mixture of mothballs and mildew. I just knew she was going to kill me and boil me up, and that I'd end up smelling like those farts in old sock water.

Martha led me into the windowless middle room, and I was surprised to see that the inner sanctum looked a lot like our place, but instead of the high riser and stick lamp that occupied our middle room, there were shelves and shelves of beautiful dolls. They were poised like a chorus line of beauties—blonde, brunette, and auburn haired, all different, all costumed in lovely dresses, capped in fancy hats over curled tresses. Some were propped on stands, while others sat, arms and legs outstretched, all smiling amiably at me.

"It vaz your birzday, yes? I heard everybody zinging, 'Happy birzday to you, happy birzday, Johanna.'" Martha imitated the singing, clapping her liver-spotted hands.

I remember thinking that this did not sound like the same woman who gave frequent performances of, "Get out, you drunken bum, you!"

Then, I noticed Martha, herself. She was wearing a kerchief around her head, with silvery-blonde rolled bangs sitting on her forehead, just like Olivia de Havilland wore in the Rosie the Riveter ads. And her dress was like one I saw in pictures of my mother when my brother Richard was a baby. On her feet were open toed, ankle strap shoes á la Joan Crawford.

I also couldn't help but notice that her toenails and fingernails were deep yellow and extremely long. Her face and teeth were a little yellow, too, but her eyes were sparkling blue and crinkling with kindness as she spoke.

"You like ze dollz, yes?"

I nodded mutely, still confused by the images of the monster upstairs I had imagined Martha to be, and the reality of this gentle old lady who lived in Toyland.

"Take one, take a doll for your birzday." She smiled, panning the shelves with her open hand.

"Really?" I found my voice.

She gestured again.

I chose a blonde, banana-curled doll in a purple satin dress with a matching plumed hat. It was the most beautiful doll I ever saw.

Martha ushered me toward the front door, and I walked out with the doll secured in my arms.

"You come again, Johanna, we have ice cream next time."

I had cookies and milk, ice cream, candy, and all those good things many times with Martha. I even had the dreaded boiling farts in old sock water, which was, in fact, cabbage soup.

She told me stories of her growing up in Germany. She showed me the only remaining photographs of the family she lost in the Holocaust. Martha, pointing at the faded pictures, described a little of how life was before Hitler tore her world apart.

She said that her father was a music teacher, and that's how she met Karl, who was studying art in the same school. She spoke of her mother, a kind woman who worked hard at their farm in a little German town. Cows and horses.

Martha played the piano, she said, but when the Nazis occupied the town, they took over the farm. I didn't understand what she was talking about, but she stopped speaking, looked down at her hands, closed her eyes for a moment, and then changed the subject to happier memories—picnics, shopping in the big city of Berlin, marveling at Karl's paintings.

She and Karl lost touch after they were taken to different camps, and it was by chance, sheer chance, that they ran into each other after the camps were liberated. Both of them lost parents, siblings, and all their relatives. They took up with each other out of need and came to America.

Martha never played the piano again. Karl never painted again. Though they were both around my mother's age (30-something), they were old inside.

Martha told me that she enjoyed hearing Frances play the piano, and I said that she could come downstairs and play it, if she wanted. She just smiled.

She never did tell me when she started collecting dolls, but perhaps their smiles and colorful costumes helped her cope. I came to understand that my mother was right when she told us to have some respect.

MY SHORT-LIVED CRIMINAL CAREER

A middle-aged woman named Dora lived right next door to us. She was born in Brooklyn but taken to Sicily as an infant. She returned at 18 and spoke with a heavy Italian accent for the rest of her life. During the times when Blackie was gone and we didn't have a phone (because it was a choice between the telephone or food), he'd call Dora's instead.

She'd tap on the wall and call out, "Frenzi, you husband on a da fone."

Dora had a husband once, whom she referred to as a "no-gooda-son-o-ma-bitch-bastardo." Dora herself told this to my mother: She threw him out years before after he tried to beat her into telling him where she hid the rent money.

She tolerated his screaming and cursing, but when he raised his fist to her, she raised a carving knife to him, demonstrating his fate should he ever come back, as she pushed him out the door. Dora was then a woman alone with 4 strong teenaged sons. They backed up her threat.

She went to work in the dress factory, the storefront beneath her apartment. She did piecework, which meant she got paid for the number of collars she was able to sew each day. She was fast on the machine and earned decent money—sometimes 30 dollars a week. Not a king's ransom, but enough to pay the rent and feed her kids. Her sons helped out, too.

If it was agreed (maybe) that Pauline was the mother of the prettiest girl on the block, then Dora's sons took the collective prize for best-looking boys. They were dead ringers for popular movie idols at the time—so much so, that very few people in the neighborhood knew their real names. They were referred to by their screen names:

"There's Errol Flynn coming home from work."

"Tyrone Power got engaged."

"Victor Mature joined the army."

"Guy Madison was out on the ledge yesterday, washing his mother's windows."

Errol Flynn's name was John. He was killed in a car crash in Florida at 24. I'll never forget that day—Dora sitting at our table, crying uncontrollably.

Visits to Dora's were consistent, if not interesting. My mother would dye Dora's gray hair and touch up her roots by wrapping a pencil with cotton and sewing thread, dipping it into a bowl filled with black dye, and applying the dye to Dora's head. While we waited for the messy process to finish, Dora would show us, over and over again, pictures of her sons, sighing and beaming with pride. They were always the same pictures, but she seemed to find something new to brag about every time.

One day, when I was about 5, Dora sensed my boredom and gave me her wooden jewelry box to play with while my mother worked on her hair, a ritual that always ended with Dora asking, "Frenzi, you make-a da freenge?" Translated: "Frances, can you cut my bangs?"

The jewelry box was brimming with all kinds of sparkling and shiny adornments, and I began to put everything on at once. Then, I spotted a ring with a dazzling red stone. All the pearls, gold chains, crystal earrings—everything, yes, everything—paled next to that ring. I had to have it. So, I put it in my pocket. I put everything else back into the box and returned to Dora's picture show.

When we got home, I paraded around, showing off the ring in all poses and directions. It turned out that not only was I a lousy wringer of clothes, but I was also a stupid robber of rings.

Frances saw it. She said nothing, took me by the hand, and marched me next door. I also said nothing, for even at the age of 5, I knew that anything I wanted to say would only add fuel to Frances' fire.

Dora opened the door, and Frances said simply, "My daughter has something to tell you."

I took the ring off my sweating finger, the same finger that, only moments before, was dancing carelessly in the air, and lay the ring in Dora's hand.

"I took it."

And that was it. Not a word was exchanged. Frances marched me back home, and it was never talked about. My mother was a woman of action, and my criminal career was out of action, forever.

JIMMY'S MOTHER

Jimmy Esposito's 85-year-old mother lived in a big house that was very much *around the corner*, far from the El. She liked nothing more than baking biscotti and conversing in Italian with her parakeet. Jimmy's mother worked hard to get everything in her lovely home. Jimmy's father had died years and years ago, and all their other children had moved away, leaving only Jimmy, who lived under the El in a railroad apartment much like ours.

Jimmy's mother worked with Dora years before in the factory—well into her 70s. Dora must have known her name, but when she spoke of her, Dora referred to her only as "Jimmy's mother." Once in a while, Frances dyed her hair, but after she retired, Jimmy's mother didn't care if it turned white.

It seems that one day, Jimmy visited his mother in her lovely, sunlit house (sunlight was standard in homes *around the corner*). She had a beautiful dining room with custom draperies, floral wallpaper, and an elegant mahogany dining suite that seated 12 (with 3 leaves). But, the dining room was for special occasions, so Jimmy and his mother sat in the kitchen. She made a pot of coffee and put out some nice biscotti for her Jimmy. Then she sat, listening in earnest, as Jimmy explained to her that it would be in her best interest to sell her house and give Jimmy all the money.

He would then purchase another house, where he would live, and, "Mama, here's the best part. I'm going to finish the basement—maybe in a nice wood paneling—and make an apartment for you. It will be beautiful. You'll be so happy there. What do you think?"

Jimmy's mother listened and nodded, and when Jimmy ended his pitch, Jimmy's mother took his hand in hers and smiled. "Okay, I'm gonna sell-a my house-a. I'm gonna give-a you all-a da money. Then, you gonna buy another house-a, and you gonna live in the house-a, and you gonna stick-a me in the bashament-a."

Jimmy said, "Yes, Mama. What do you think?"

Jimmy's mother leaned forward and said, "You know, Jimmy, this make-a no god-a-damn-a sense to me."

Jimmy thought that since his mother spent her time talking to a parakeet, she, too, must have had a bird-sized brain.

SHAKE AND SNIFF

Across the street, on the other side of the El, we had whom we called "The Shaker." The apartment she lived in had its entrance on 80th Street, but her clothesline faced New Utrecht Avenue. I think her name was Mary. She used to wash her clothes by hand, on the scrub board, just like us, then hang them on her very own clothesline. She didn't have to share.

Mary would shake every garment a million times. Each time, she'd sniff it—every inch—shake it again, sniff, shake, sniff, shake, and, finally, the dizzy shirts and unsteady underwear were pinned to the clothesline. She was a hoot.

The Shaker used to air out her bed linens every day, just as Frances did, but with less soot flying around. Same routine: shake and sniff, shake and sniff, then pin. I don't know if Frances ever visited her. I just used to see them wave at each other from across the street.

Speaking of windows, Frances used to wash the windows (all 6 of them) every Saturday. Using newspaper dipped in a mixture of water and vinegar, she'd sit on the window's ledge while Joseph held on to her legs in desperation.

"You're going to fall!"

MILLIE ADAMS

Chuck and Millie Adams lived *around the corner*. I didn't know what Chuck did for a living, but Millie had babies. They only had 4 kids, but at the time, it seemed like there was always a new baby the Adams' house.

Their son Patrick, the oldest of the four, was my age, and we played cards in their middle room. I taught him to play poker, another useful thing Blackie handed down to me besides reading the racing form to handicap horses and how to play blackjack. Blackie was an excellent gin rummy player and could've made a good living at it, in addition to his regular cab driver gig. Pity that he hardly brought the money home. We shouldn't have had to live in the dark.

Frances liked Millie. They were friendly—and Frances didn't make new friends. Her friendships were cemented years before; it was a very small circle. Frances also had no time for a coffee klatch.

When Millie came for visits, it wasn't to gossip about the neighbors; it was to sew or knit and talk about the new Butterick or Simplicity patterns, or what color wool to use for her newest baby's sweater. Sure, they had coffee (and cigarettes), but that was done in between the "knit one, purl two" stitch or while threading the bobbin on the old Singer. "Idle hands are the devil's playground" was one of my mother's mottos.

Frances never went to Millie's place because she had as many cats as she had children, and my mother had asthma, and people with asthma, she said, could not be around cats. The truth was, as we came to learn later, my mother hated cats because they jumped on the table while people were eating. Millie's clothes were always loaded with cat hair, as was her apartment.

Millie didn't care much for cleaning, but she liked to paint, so when there was an occasion in the family, like a birthday or christening, she'd paint the entire apartment to freshen up the place. But, the painting parties ended and the babies stopped coming when Chuck ran off with a 20-year-old waitress—or so the story goes.

With my father on the lam and Chuck off with the waitress, there should've been a lot of husband bashing going on, but never a word was said by either woman about either man. In their common circumstance, there was an unspoken reasoning that it's better not to talk about things you can't do anything about. They just continued...knit one, purl two. Oops, I dropped a stitch!

CHAPTER SEVEN
PLAYMATES

I was not a girly girl. I played with the boys. I had my first real date at 15, and my mother had to holler out the window for me to come home and get ready.

"What are you doing playing football in the street? When are you going to act like a lady?"

Like all kids of the 1950s and 1960s, we played most of our games outside. Some didn't even have names. Just run, catch a ball, bounce a ball, hit a ball, tag each other, run some more. Run, catch, play...until your mother yelled your name from the window of your house to come home for supper. I remember one kid whose mother did it Italian style.

"Filippe, vieni a mangiare!" (Filippe, come eat!)

Dora and her handsome sons lived on one side of us. Sharing the plasterboard on the other side was a young couple. They had a son that they called Charlie Boy. I didn't know their names and instead referred to them and addressed them as Charlie Boy's mother and father. Charlie Boy and I were the same age, and given the proximity of our living arrangements, we played together.

I'd ring his bell and holler in the hallway, from the bottom of the steps, "Charlie Boy's mother, can Charlie

Boy come out and play?"

Or, he'd yell up to my mother, "Joanne's mother, can Joanne come out and play?"

Charlie Boy and I played street games like Kick the Can, Hide and Seek, and Red Light Green Light, or we'd just pull each other's hair. When I was 6 years old, I had a set of pop beads (little pastel colored plastic balls that fit into each other) that I used to make a necklace. Charlie Boy thought it would be fun if we disassembled the necklace and put the pop beads in my mouth, just to see if I could fit them all in. I accidentally swallowed one, and Charlie Boy told me that I was going to die.

"I'm not gonna die!"

But, Charlie Boy knew better. "Oh, yes, pop beads are poison, and you're gonna die."

Then, Charlie Boy told me his plan. If I got off the block and went somewhere else, God would not be able to find me, and He'd forget about me, and He'd forget about the poisonous pop bead slowly killing me, and I wouldn't die. Then, when God completely forgot, it would be safe for me to return. It was my only chance, swore Charlie Boy on a stack of bibles.

"I'll go with you," he said, and we were off.

We walked *around the corner* and crossed more than 10 streets. Two 6-year-olds on the lam from God, one with a poison pop bead in her stomach.

We started to get hungry. We passed a candy store, and Charlie Boy bought 3 pretzel sticks with a nickel he found in his pocket. We kept on walking, and when it started to get dark, I began to see the light.

"You're full of baloney. I'm not going to die. I'm going home!"

Charlie Boy laughed and laughed, pointing at me, "You believed me! You believed me!"

When we got to our block, where the El meets *around the corner*, Charlie stopped laughing. A crowd of people was standing around, grouped to form a united front, exchanging nervous shrugs and looking like they just heard bad news on the radio. Everyone was there: Millie Adams, Carmelina, Sally, Dora, Big Mouth Pauline, Charlie Boy's mother—and Frances.

Frances was wearing her maroon suit with matching pumps, an outfit she saved for special occasions. Her blonde hair was pulled back in her customary Faye Emerson chignon, but it seemed tighter than usual. Her lips were drawn tighter than her hairdo. Her arms were folded. She was staring at me.

As Charlie Boy and I walked through the crowd, Big Mouth Pauline whispered into my ear, "Your mother went to the police. She is going to kill you!"

Charlie Boy's mother ran toward us, crying, "Thank God, thank God," and scooped up Charlie Boy into her grateful arms. Then, she looked at me and said, "Where did you take my son, you little brat?"

I just stood there, dumbfounded, but Charlie Boy's mother was the very least of my problems. I smelled Frances. I looked up, and there she was, a 5' giant stewed in Chanel No. 5. Then came the drill.

She took my hand, and we marched, in silence, out of the crowd. We marched away from where the El meets *around the corner*, marched past Charlie Boy's door, marched into our smelly hallway, and marched up the stairs to our landing. When we got inside the door—HALT!

Then, the bubble broke. Frances let loose. "Don't you *ever* go off this block again!"

She reached for one of my father's leather belts that hung from a hook in our only closet. I tried to run and hide under her bed but only got as far as the *abranda*.

With every stroke of the belt, she pronounced, "When I decide (smack) to let you (smack) go out again, you'll stay (smack) right in front of this house (smack) where I can see you!"

In between the smacks and defensive moves, I tried to explain, "Charlie Boy told me I was going to die because I ate a pop bead, and I had to run away!"

She stopped the belting, and the disappointment on her face was worse than the smack of the belt. "And you believed him?" Then she sighed, "Joanne, I hope you smarten up before you grow up."

THE KIDS AROUND THE CORNER

The "upper class" girls lived *around the corner*, even though their apartments were attached to the pie, and we shared the same dismal courtyard. Cathy (Big Mouth Pauline's daughter), Emelia, and Francine were a year or 2 older than me. They didn't—wouldn't ever—play with me.

Joey D'Anna, Cathy's brother, was one of my earliest memories of a playmate. He used to have regular doctor visits to my dolls. I'd bring my dolls downstairs, we'd sit on the ground, and he'd examine Tiny Tears, Betsy Wetsy, and a 2-foot lifelike toddler doll, Anna. I got her name from the game we called A, My Name Is Anna. You'd start by bouncing a ball, then swinging a leg over the ball, keeping in play, until the alphabet was exhausted. I was always worn out before we got to "H, my name is Helen."

"A, my name is Anna, and my husband's name is Al. We live in Alabama, and we sell apples." Bounce, leg, bounce, leg.

I'll leave it to your imagination as to what an 8-year-old boy doll doctor thought was proper treatment for his plastic patients.

Cathy was, as I wrote, considered the prettiest girl on our pie-shaped block. Emelia thought she was, but if truth be told, it was Francine Dasaro who was the prettiest girl on the entire pie. Emelia was a snob, just like her mother. Big Mouth Pauline was what Jewish people call a *yente*—a gossip and a busybody—who couldn't wait to report me to my mother for any perceived infraction I committed.

Francine's mother, Mary, was a gem. Beautiful, petite, a little on the nervous side, she was always so wonderful to me, in contrast to Emelia's mother, who looked at me like I just climbed out of a sewer. Emelia's brother, Raymond, was the snot-nose that got my brother almost beaten to death.

I suppose my most cherished memory of a playmate belongs to Francine's brother, Jackie (née Steven) Dasaro. He and his beautiful sister, fabulous mother, and miniature poodle, Charlie, moved to *around the corner* when I was 9. They also had a little brother, Dennis, whom I never really got to know.

Mary and her husband separated in the early '60s, and to make extra money, she'd man the phones for the local bookies. Mary used her own phone and was paid 60 dollars a month, plus the cost of the phone bill. If she had to leave to go shopping, Jackie and I would take the calls.

One day, 3 police cars pulled up in front of her apartment, sirens blaring. Six—count them, 6—cops with guns drawn flew up the stairs and dragged the 5', 95 pound Mary out, under arrest, for racketeering. Her only concern was that New York's finest didn't let her take the rollers out of her hair and change her clothes from a bathrobe and furry slippers into something more fashionable for her mug shot.

Jackie taught me how to dance. And, he encouraged me to be svelte. He offered me a new pair of bell-bottom pants if I lost 20 pounds. We practiced all the dances in my apartment after school: the shing-a-ling, the Boston monkey, the cha-cha, the tango, and our favorite, the mambo.

In the mid-1960s, we'd go to Greenwich Village to Cafe Wha?, where on Wednesday nights, the King of Latin Music, Tito Puente, and his band performed. Every week, Jackie and I were invited to do our number on the stage.

Closer to home, Jackie and I entertained the residents at the local (one and only in those days) nursing home by doing a tango to "The Rain in Spain" from *My Fair Lady*. Whenever Jackie dipped me, he'd cry, "Hernia!" The old folks (I'm one of them now... yikes!) loved us. We brought them gifts of talcum powder and soap.

We also went to Brooklyn's Fox Theatre for the Murray the K show to see a lineup of the singers and bands for the day. For 5 dollars, we stayed for at least 5 shows. Blackie would drop us off at 1:00 in the morning (I don't remember how we reached Blackie at that time, since he was already on the lam), and we'd wait on the sidewalk until 9:00 a.m. for the 1st show. Two 15-year-old kids enjoying the likes of Stevie Wonder, Patti LaBelle and The Bluebelles, and Marvin Gaye—all for 5 dollars. Those days are gone forever.

An interjection here, since I'm writing about bands. I, along with a couple of classmates, were among the frenzied teens at JFK airport when The Beatles arrived in February 1964. I also waited in a mob to get tickets to see them at Shea Stadium. Never mistake a mob with a crowd. This was a mob. People were jumping on cars to escape being trampled. The police had to break it up. We got our tickets. Couldn't hear a thing at Shea.

Jackie took me to his high school senior prom. He told me that he hoped we'd marry some day, and he gave me a copy of his yearbook photo. On the back, it said: *To Joanne, who knows what our future holds? Love,*

Jackie (Steve). He added a drawing of an engagement ring.

But, we didn't have a future together. He became a go-go dancer at Trude Heller's in Manhattan then moved to LA to pursue a dancing career. His life was cut short at age 40. In the fall of 1987, I visited Mary at the dress shop on 86th Street where she worked, and she held me close in her arms, sobbed, and said that she was relieved that he wasn't suffering anymore.

She added, "Oh, how I wish he married you. None of this would've have happened."

Over the years, before Jackie moved away, Mary would practically plan the wedding. She told me that I would be the perfect wife for him—a nice, pretty Italian girl from the block that knew how to cook and who was respectful to her elders.

To some people, like my very intuitive mother, it was clear that Jackie would never marry a woman. I don't think Mary knew. I don't think Jackie knew when we were kids in the 1950s. It was the late 60s when Jackie, the dancer, came into his own. But, I thank you, Mary. You would have been the perfect mother-in-law.

When I was 9, the girls *around the corner* invited me to go to Ravenhall Pool in Coney Island. Cathy's parents had a locker there, which meant they were members. It was expensive. I never liked the water, especially water that smelled like chlorine—and heaven knows what else was added from the bathers.

When we were done swimming and getting our clothes, preparing to leave, I looked around and noticed that everyone was gone. No Cathy. No Cathy's father (who drove us there). No snippy Emelia. I was alone.

I left Ravenhall, went out to the street, and found a cop on the corner by the original Nathan's restaurant. I told him the story, and he gave me 15 cents for the El to go home. I didn't have the nerve to ask for another 15 cents to buy a hot dog, which was calling out my name from the Nathan's grill.

When I got to my stop on 79th Street, I saw Cathy standing outside her house. I walked over to her and punched her in the face, knocking her to the ground. A little bit of Frances comes out in me when needed.

Teresa L. was my friend from *around the corner*. She was a sweet girl, timid, and a most unlikely friend. She should have been a nun. I remember that her spinster aunt lived with her family. I know that, because that's how the woman was described—"our spinster aunt."

My mother bought me a gold ring with a pearl on it for my 9th grade graduation from Teresa's dad, Carlo, who was able to get "stuff that fell off the truck." In 1970, Carlo met his unfortunate end at the hands of people no one should mess with. End of story.

Linda B. was a school chum. We were in the same class for a couple of years and walked home together. My mother used to give me 15 cents to buy a loaf of Italian bread from Modica's bakery on the way home from school. I managed (probably by turning in bottles) to garner another 15 cents for an extra loaf, which I would eat while walking home. I'd always give Linda a nice, big piece.

One day, Linda told me that her mother didn't want her to walk with me anymore because she was getting too fat. What did I care? I had the whole loaf to myself.

I had another friend, M., who lived way, way *around the corner*, closer to the candy store, where we bought the newspapers and ice cream. She came from a Catholic school, St. Athanasius, I think, to Public School 201, my junior high school. M. was an obedient, straight-laced girl who obeyed her mother and wouldn't think of stepping out of the box.

Her mother was a beauty, as I recall, and was very kind to me. She always invited me in for dinner. I think she thought of me as a stray cat. Her father fixed our water heater once. It took him all day, but when my mother offered him money, he refused.

Her family lived in a single-family home. It was the first time, except for Aunt Tillie's house, that I'd seen all the actual "living," like cooking, having meals, and watching TV, done in the basement. The top floors were for sleeping.

M. and I lost touch, but if there's one person I will never forget, it's her little sister. Never. Dorothy was an amazing little girl. There was a 12-year age gap between M. and Dorothy. She tagged along with us 14-year-olds, and her favorite line was, "I'm going with you. Mommy said I could."

And, so she did—to the movies, to Coney Island, to the park. In 1991, Dorothy was killed in an instant by a speeding drunk driver, as she sat in the back of a taxicab. Some things are hard to take.

Another girl I'll never forget is Olivia from 18th Avenue. Blonde, beautiful, and everyone's little sister. There were a bunch of guys that hung out at the other place, Mary's candy store (really, a kind of luncheonette with tables and chairs) on 18th Avenue and 81st Street, who fed the jukebox constantly. Their hormones were always raging, but Olivia was never a target. They protected her.

It is now decades later, and the guys have scattered—none too far away, some gone forever—but Olivia is still cherished. I hope she knows that.

Kathy C. was my classmate from grade school. The first time I visited her house, her mother confronted me with, "I hope you're wearing clean bloomers—we don't let anyone in with dirty underwear. Are you wearing clean bloomers?"

Mrs. C. stood in the doorway of a brick colonial home, a home preceded by a broad and long and lush lawn. Maybe she was kidding me. After all, she was smiling.

I smiled, too, a narrow one. "Yes, I'm wearing clean bloomers."

Actually, I wasn't sure if it had been 3 days or 4 since my underwear were relieved of duty, and I couldn't be sure if my farts were dry. Kathy and her smiling mother were so rich, I doubted they ever farted.

Kathy and I were in the same class for 4th and 5th grade. She never spoke to me during the entire 4th grade. Sometime in the 5th, she heard that I wrote Joey D'Anna's book report on *Johnny Tremain*. Evidently, she was having trouble with *The Scarlet Letter* and started talking to me in the schoolyard one day.

She came to my house (we all referred to where we lived as our "house," even if it was an apartment—or even a tent), and after about 5 minutes, she teased me about the "shithole" I lived in. Apparently, she told her mother, and her mother jumped on the teasing wagon with her clean bloomer question.

One day, we were in her basement (which was used for entertainment purposes only) blowing up balloons for her birthday party. We got silly and filled them with water, and we started giggling threats of tossing them at each other. Mine broke, and the water fell onto the expensive bar. She cursed me out and told me to go back to the s-hole where I belonged. I swung my fist at her face, hitting her nose. I left with Kathy trying to keep the blood away from the teak wood.

The other time I had to defend the cold water flat was when a nice boy invited me to his junior prom in 1962. One of the tough girls, Pat M., whose house, from the outside, looked like it could fit an army, told me to meet the boy at the prom, and that I shouldn't let him see that shit-box I lived in.

By this point, I had a solid right hook. I left her

bleeding on 12th Avenue and 81st Street.

The next day in the schoolyard, Pat, donning a swollen nose, threatened to get some tough girls from Red Hook to teach me a lesson. Yep, I was scared.

We had one Black girl in our class, Reatha, who basically stayed to herself, but she and I would occasionally say hello or nod to each other in the hallways. She overheard Pat's threat and said to me, "I like you. Don't worry—I got you covered. Nothing will happen to you."

And, that was the end of Pat's lesson.

Rosalie lived across 81st Street but still under the El—though it never felt like the El was there because she lived in a real house with all the *around the corner* amenities. Her mother, as I recall, was a beautiful redhead who drove a convertible. Rosalie and I played records on her Victrola. One of our favorites was Elvis singing "Don't Be Cruel." Every time Elvis moaned, we put the needle back to hear it over and over.

One day, I noticed a spot of blood in my underwear, and her mother gave me a Modess disposable pad. I'd never seen one. When I'd had my first period at age 9 and a half, my mother, overjoyed that I became a lady, gave me cut-up cloth diapers to use. I had to wash them on the scrub board and use them again and again. When I saw the Modess, I went home and told my mother that I wanted to be like Rosalie and wear the pads that get thrown out. Frances bought me a box. It came with the belt and safety pins to keep the pad in place. That made me feel like a lady!

Other friends and acquaintances came and went, and such is life. Time changes everything, and all those cute little "May our friendship never end" or "Good luck in High School" notes in our graduation diaries mostly amounted to empty words and—years later—trying to figure out who it was that wrote them.

THE JANITOR OF JUSTICE

Now, it was clear to everyone under the El and *around the corner* that, should you mess with Frances, she'd wipe the streets with you. And, Frances was economical when it came to words. She made her point quickly and was fond of saying, "Talk is cheap." Frances let actions speak for her.

Once, when she was in the 7th grade (there was 7A and 7B, a 6-month term, not a full year), she lost her hat and asked the teacher to help her find it.

The teacher shrugged and said, "Why bother? The hat was probably only worth 2 cents."

Frances walked quietly back to her seat, picked up the filled glass inkwell, and threw it at the teacher. She crowned the teacher, and Frances was left back and had to repeat the 7A term—a common punishment way back when teachers decided a student's fate. Today, we'd call it "left behind."

"It was worth it," she said when telling the story. She'd do it again in a minute.

Let's not forget that my mother once dragged a woman by her hair from a dance hall into the street after the woman flirted with Blackie, stating, "He's with me."

Not long after my father had come home from parts unknown, after 6 years, a woman rang the bell.

"Is Joe there?"

Frances answered the buzzer. "Joe? There's no Joe here."

The woman replied, "I mean Blackie."

"Who wants to know?" my mother asked. Frances leaned over the banister to get a better look at the woman asking for my father. She looked like Sophie

Tucker with black roots. Frances shouted, "You came to the wrong house, lady. Now, get lost!"

Miss Tucker held her ground. "I'm not leaving until I talk to Joe."

"You'll talk to me!" Frances flew down the stairs, pounced on the woman, and pulled a sizeable chunk of blonde hair out of her black-rooted head. Frances then opened the front door and kicked Miss Tucker's sizeable ass into the street.

My brothers and I ran to the bedroom window and leaned out to get front ledge seats. We watched in awe as Frances spun her around by her collar then knocked the Tucker woman down, several times. She tried to fight back, but she did not stand a chance, even though she was twice the size of Frances.

Sophie Tucker limped off like a wounded buffalo with black and blonde hair, never to return. When we told my father what happened, he laughed.

"Your mother is a wild woman."

Not another word was said. Case closed. That gives some background as to my mother's wrath, if unleashed.

Joseph used to play with the Puerto Rican boy that lived around the corner, next door to the Adams family. His name, as we pronounced it, was Poochie. One day, his mother slapped Joseph. Big Mouth Pauline couldn't wait to tell Frances, just to see what would happen—and hopefully give the block a free floorshow. Upon hearing the news, Frances removed the apron she had been wearing, neatly folded it, and, like a soldier marching to meet the enemy, went to the house of the slapper.

"Come down here. Don't let me come up there and get you."

The woman told Frances to go to hell.

Frances climbed the 2 flights, stopping at the 1st landing. "I'm coming up!"

Frances arrived at the door and pushed it open.

She grabbed that woman by her hair (a brunette, this time) and dragged her down those 2 flights and into the street, where she wiped 17th Avenue with her. Everyone from Joe the Butcher (who dropped dead on the same day that Marilyn Monroe left the world) to Joe the Barber (who stunk from here to high heaven) watched Frances, the Janitor of Justice, make her case in public.

One of the sidewalk audience members asked Frances why she didn't just take care of the woman when she went upstairs.

Frances replied, "It's against the law to hit someone in her own house."

OTHER GAMES AND SPORTS

As I mentioned, my brother Richard and I played marbles in the slanted foyer at 8018, but he also played in the schoolyard at Public School 204 in the only patch of dirt behind the building. The rest of the surrounding area was concrete.

In all the public schools I attended (PS 204 and PS 201, which our graduating class named Dyker Heights Junior High), there were games, made up or otherwise, in the yards. We played catch, or Monkey in the Middle. We also played handball against the concrete walls that were designed just for that game. Does anyone play handball anymore?

New Utrecht High School (NUHS) had grass and a quarter-mile track. That's where Richard taught me to ride a bike, all around the track on that secondhand bike given to me by Joe Colombo.

At NUHS, there was a pool with compulsory swimming. They gave us woolen bathing suits that didn't fit. For the girls who were "developed" like me, it was a nightmare. I did not want to get in the pool, and I pleaded "that time of the month" every week.

Mrs. Scher, the swimming teacher, warned us, "I don't care how often you get your period. You better be able to swim at the end of the term, or I'll fail you."

I had no problem.

Swim class had an additional perk—if you can call it a perk. There were always boys sneaking in to watch the girls change. And, there were girls who thought it was funny to steal the other girls' clothes.

As I mentioned, Frances loved to swim, almost as much as Aunt Louise. Frances would have loved to have been a member of the Polar Bears, who swam in the ocean all year round. As it was, she'd walk Joseph and me in the stroller to Coney Island in the winter, all along the boardwalk in the freezing cold. It was good for us, she said.

"Clean, fresh ocean air. Best thing for you."

In summers, she took us to the beach and taught us to swim in the waves of Coney's saltwater. She packed lunch. While other kids were eating hot dogs and knishes, we had salami sandwiches on Wonder Bread, heated by the relentless sun, laced with sand that seeped into the bag, so they always tasted more like the sand and less like the salami.

The most humiliating part of the day was when we were getting ready to leave. Frances would wrap a tiny towel around me, peel off my bathing suit, and hand me my underwear and dress. I would look all around to see if anyone was looking while I rushed to get the clothes on my damp skin. I hated it then, hate it now. Haven't worn a bathing suit in 50 years.

In the 1960s, basketball was not a big sport in Bensonhurst, but when I revisited NUHS in the early '90s, I noticed that the track was gone—replaced with an outdoor basketball court and AstroTurf. The pool was gone, as were the doors on the stalls in the girls bathroom. There were bars on the windows, and there was graffiti everywhere.

But, the school's motto was still carved at the front entrance: WHEREVER LAW ENDS, TYRANNY BEGINS, written by John Locke.

We were very inventive kids—without the use of electronic technology. For example, we made our own "carpet guns." Take 2 sticks—one long, one short. Hammer a nail into the top of the long stick at the front. Attach the short stick to the back of the long stick so that the finished product looks like a gun. Attach a big rubber band to the nail. Steal some linoleum from the hallways and break it into pieces. Hold the carpet piece inside the rubber band, pull, and let go. Sounds complicated, but it wasn't. Certainly no Operation Moon Base!

One of the most terrific childhood inventions was the "scooter." Take an orange crate and attach it to a long, sturdy stick in the front. Keep the open part of the crate facing back. Attach 2 shorter sticks on the top of the crate to resemble handlebars. The scoot part comes from taking apart a roller skate and nailing 2 wheels in the front of the stick and 2 wheels in the back. To create a trim, hammer bottle caps into the crate in any design you think is cool. To me, the whole thing was cool. It was the grandfather to the skateboard, but we built it ourselves.

The winters under the El gave us different sports. We climbed the mountains of snow and slid down into oncoming traffic. The schools were rarely closed for snow, even if it was 4 feet deep. We just stomped through and never thought about staying home. On those freezing, snowy days, the girls were allowed to wear pants under our dresses and then take them off in the classroom. When the schools did close, it was like

Mardi Gras in New Orleans.

We built snowmen, as all kids do. We threw snowballs at each other. The best balls came from snow that was really packed. We stayed out all day, if the schools were closed. On regular snowy days, we couldn't wait to get home from school to go out again and play until suppertime.

There was the street facing NUHS yard that was perfect for "sledding." Nobody had a sled. We took a side of a refrigerator box (or any big, rectangular piece of cardboard) and lay flat on it. We'd give it a little push, starting from 79th Street, and go down to 80th Street. Then, we'd drag the cardboard back and do it over and over.

One day, Joseph hit a nail that was on the sidewalk, and it ripped open his calf. My mother was working, and I had to think fast. I stopped a car and asked the driver to take us to the Coney Island hospital. Joseph was bleeding a lot. The man gave us a rag from the trunk of his car to wrap it. When we got to the hospital, the doctor came out and told me that I needed a parent there in order to treat my bleeding brother.

I lied and told him that my father was waiting outside. "I'll go get him." I ran up to the first man I saw outside the hospital and said, "You're my father. Please, come with me. Remember, you're my father. Your name is Joseph De Simone. Your son, Joseph, is in there."

We could NEVER get away with that now, but it worked. Joseph was stitched up, and "Dad" went on his way. I called Blackie at the cabstand, a kind of office where we could leave messages for the cabbies that worked for that taxi company. I still remember the phone number (GE8-1100).

I left a message for him. Joseph and I waited at the hospital for about an hour, and then Blackie showed up and took us home. My mother told me that I was very smart and "thought on my feet." Since she wasn't yelling or throwing anything at me, I took it as a compliment, but I didn't know what my feet had to do with it.

The air is different now in the neighborhood. It used to smell like home. Now, it just smells like the past, like L&B Spumoni Gardens pizza, or Alba's pastry shop, or the ball for all seasons, Spaulding (or "Spaldeens"), or my mother's perfume. All gone now.

It takes a passing breeze or an occasional visit to awaken the sense of smell and bring it all back. Remember what was written about Toyland? "Once you pass its borders, you can never return again."

CHAPTER EIGHT
WHEN MANDRAKE DISAPPEARED

Blackie worked nights driving a cab in New York City, leaving the house about 3:30 in the afternoon and coming home around 4:00 in the morning—if he came home, that is. On very cold nights, or during rain or snowstorms, I'd wait by the window and watch for him. I couldn't sleep, thinking of him out there, cold or wet. I wanted him to be home, safe, warm.

Some nights, my mother would find me with my head on the windowsill, asleep, and put me back to bed. Other nights, I'd hear the key in the door and rush to meet him, pulling his arm, leading him to my room. I'd throw all my dolls out of the bed to make room for Blackie.

He'd tuck me in, brush my hair back with his fingers, and sing, *"I'll be loving you always, with a love that's true always, not for just an hour, not for just a day, not for just a year, but always."*

In the morning, my dolls were back on the bed with me. I'd quickly look through the curtain (yes, no door—just a flowery print curtain between rooms) into my parents' room, just to be sure that Blackie was home. I was assured when I saw his trousers hanging on the bedpost and further assured seeing his head of jet-black hair on the pillow next to Frances.

He slept while we were in school and was gone well before dinnertime. No, Blackie was never around for the "father" stuff, like Open School Night, where the teachers met the parents to discuss the students' progress. Blackie didn't even know if I went to school or not. And, as far as my teachers knew, my father was a phantom—or, as my uncle Rico called him, Mandrake the Magician—living life in acts of appearances and disappearances...now you see him, now you don't. And, that's the kind of father he was. A kind of freelancer.

When he was home, he was attentive, funny, charming, and loving. Sometimes, he'd stay away for a night or 2. But, he always came back, bearing small gifts and full of funny stories. It was all quite normal. Once in a while, he'd take us to Coney Island, but it was with one foot off the carousel and one eye on his watch. There was always a horse race or a card game (or a woman) waiting.

My girlfriends loved Blackie. In the half hour from the time I came home from school until Blackie left for work, he'd entertain us—teasing my friends, telling stories in foreign accents, singing silly songs. It was just a half hour, but Blackie, the true showman, gave them just enough to keep them coming back, just as he gave his wife and family enough of a show to want him around. Blackie's greatest trick was getting everyone to love him.

It was in November 1960, when I was 11 years old, that my father went on the lam. He owed bookies from the "four corners," meaning the boroughs of Brooklyn, Queens, Manhattan, and the Bronx—a combined total of close to a quarter-million dollars.

In the middle of a chilly night, his routine was abnormal, even for Blackie. He didn't come to my bed to sit with me, nor brush my hair back with his hand, nor sing to me. He woke my brothers and me, abruptly, and told us to come to the dining room. His tone was strange. It was immediately apparent that he wasn't planning one of his usual midnight surprises of bringing home a stray dog or a lost turtle. My mother was seated at the table, crying openly—which, for Frances, was just as unusual as laughing openly.

Without any explanation, and without conversation, he told us he was leaving and that he was not coming back. Then, he asked us, one by one, if we wanted to stay with my mother, or go with him. Standing barefoot in our pajamas, in the middle of the dining room, in the middle of the night, cold, confused and bewildered, my brothers and I looked at each other. In cracked, frightened voices, we whispered, individually, that we wanted to stay with our mother. Or, maybe we just didn't want to get out of our pajamas and get dressed to go out into the cold night.

Though it's true that even in the best of times, Blackie would never win the Father of the Year award, he certainly had no rivals for Mr. Congeniality. But, the man that spoke to us in that dimly lit room, while my mother sobbed, holding her hands over her face, was not my father. This was not the man who told me I was beautiful. This was not my father, who, even as a part-time dad, was tender and affectionate, who softly sang to me "I'll Be Loving You Always" and "Daddy's Little Girl." It was not possible. This Blackie announced that if we wanted to stay with Frances, we were no longer his children, and if we ever saw him on the street, we were to pretend not to know him.

He walked toward the door but turned sharply back to my mother and roughly tore the eyeglasses from her face. "I'll take these. I paid for them!"

My mother sat, shaking and squinting, gulping back the choking flood of tears, her naked face white.

Richard ran to her; Joseph stood, crouched over, crying and holding his stomach; I advanced on my father like a terrier.

"You can't take Mommy's glasses. She can't see without them. Please, please, give them back!"

Blackie tossed the glasses to me, turned, and walked down the dark stairs into the night. He was gone.

After Mandrake disappeared, life in the apartment under the El was not just its usual dark. It was shadowed in mystery, as if another El went up around us. We knew neither why Blackie left, nor why he fled like a thief in the night. And, why was he so cruel? We never found out. Frances did not speak to us about it, nor did she comfort us about the absence of our father.

The presence of my freelance father was gravely missed. There were no more silly songs or funny stories. In fact, nothing was funny.

My brothers and I were not permitted to tell anyone that Blackie was not living at home. Frances gave us strict instructions with a tight-lipped, determined warning that if anyone asked about him, we were to say that Blackie works nights. And, if anyone questioned it, we were to tell Frances, and she would "straighten them out."

Months passed. No word from Blackie. He hadn't even called on December 1 to say happy birthday. I had a "Happy Birthday Daddy" card for him, which I kept under my pillow in hopes that he would come home one night and we would celebrate. But the card became wrinkled and dog-eared and finally found its way to the top drawer of my dresser where it sat, lost among other cards, papers, and junk, for 6 years.

On those terrible rainy or snowy nights, I kept vigil at the window, anxious, crying silently, praying that he would come home, out of the bad weather. Home safe, sitting on my bed, stroking my hair. Sometimes, I heard sniffling coming from my mother's bed.

When I'd ask her what was the matter, she'd call out, "I have a cold...go to bed, or you'll catch one, too!"

CHAPTER NINE
MONEY AND OTHER
EATING DISORDERS

Before Blackie left, money was never abundant, but Frances managed to put food on the table, and we all had new shoes at the start of the school year. After Blackie left, the dollar had to be stretched, so shoes and clothes had to make do longer with the aid of shoe polish and carpet remnants, and meals became somewhat "institutionalized."

We still had macaroni and meatballs on Sunday, but the meatballs were made from one pound of ground beef mixed with a one-pound bag of breadcrumbs. The weekday menu consisted of macaroni and beans, macaroni and peas, macaroni and chickpeas, macaroni and broccoli, and—to vary the starch intake—on Fridays, rice and tomato sauce. Saturdays' fare was potato and egg sandwiches.

The seltzer man who delivered U-Bet chocolate syrup along with seltzer had to be discontinued, so no more homemade chocolate sodas or egg creams. We also had to ignore the cries of the fish man on Friday mornings, who sold fish from a pushcart on the street and yelled up to the windows, "*Pesce, pesce!*" (Fish, fish!).

We could still have our knives sharpened because the knife and scissor man didn't charge anything. I'm not sure how much cutting power we needed to hack through the macaroni and peas, but as long as it was free, why not have sharp knives around?

When most of the food that ends up on the table begins with, "Put it on my bill," at the grocery store, dining is just eating—a matter of survival. It's hardly a bill of fare. It is more like an eating disorder.

In the 1950s, cash was the only tender—at least on my block. And, for our family, cash was not always available. So, we ate on credit. In modern times, people do it every day. We're able to dine for hours at a restaurant, and the bill can soar, and no one knows if you can pay for it. That's what credit cards are for—buying things you can't afford. But, in the '50s, credit wasn't fashionable or chic, and it wasn't advertised as a shiny pocket-sized card with my mother's name proudly embossed on the bottom. Our credit card was a black composition book on a string that hung from a hook behind the store's counter—a book filled with names of people buying "on the bill," each of them with a page dedicated to their running account.

My mother's name was scribbled on a page with a number 2 pencil. The pencil was a good sign. It meant that she might pay the bill someday, and the debt would be erased, and so would all the shame. We were "booked" in every store in the neighborhood—the grocer, the butcher, the baker, the druggist.

Food was not fancy. It couldn't be. Imagine Frances asking the butcher for filet mignon and then asking him to put it on the bill. We ate chopped meat, or what is now called ground beef. The new description is to ensure the customer that there is, in fact, beef involved. It's like eating steak—just ground up. I'm not sure what we ate, but if it was on credit, it probably used to be on the floor, or in a stable.

After Blackie left, Frances bought more and more stuff from "the Jew," Mr. Krantz (and one other man, whose name escapes me.) The Jew sold dry goods door-to-door, things such as towels, sheets, blouses, socks, and underwear. Frances bought on credit and paid one dollar a week on account. Every Sunday morning, the Jew would come around to collect his dollar.

When we heard the knock on the door, one of us little bastards would holler out, "Ma, it's the Jew!"

My mother spoke to both men in Yiddish. If she didn't have the buck to pay them, they never pressed her.

"It's all right. You pay me when you have a chance."

For groceries, Frances sent us to Sal's Market, a traditional grocery store that sold everything from canned goods to cough medicine. It was the kind of place with sawdust on the floor and shelves all the way to the ceiling. Sal had one of those sticks with the metal grabbers on the end to retrieve cans and boxes from the upper shelves.

We never went there with money. Instead, Frances told us to tell Sal to put it on the bill. Others had one page in the black book. Our section usually ran to 3 pages. Sal would bag our groceries and log the amount in the book.

Very often, he'd whisper to me, "Ask your mother to come see me when she has a chance."

When things got tight, Frances would borrow money from one of the fellas from the Café Espresso. These guys were loan sharks. We called them "Shys," short for Shylock. Frances had to pay 30 dollars a week until the loan was paid in full. The 30 dollars was not applied to the principle. It was considered interest, over and above the principle. When the 300 dollars was paid, in full, all at once, the 30 a week stopped. They weren't called sharks for nothing. There were times Frances would send me with 10 of the required 30.

The Shy would take the 10 and whisper, "Ask your mother to come see me when she has a chance."

Things even tighter, Frances found a lending company called Beneficial Finance that had a small office down the street, above one of the stores. With Beneficial Finance, the interest was applied to the principle, but the interest was about 30 percent. They were just loan sharks with an office and a listed phone number. She would borrow the 300 and pay the Shy in full. Then the phone calls would start.

Once, when Frances was outside sweeping the sidewalk, I yelled out the window, "Ma, Beneficial Finance is on the phone!"

She ran up the stairs, hit me with the broom, and snapped, "When they call me, you refer to them as Benny, not Beneficial Finance."

So, from then on, the neighbors thought she had a boyfriend named Benny. Better to have been known as an adulteress than a deadbeat.

Benny called all the time, saying, "Ask your mother to call me when she has a chance."

On September 30, 1964, I hosted a party. I baked a cake, and on it, it read, "Happy 25th Anniversary, Frances and Gi." I bought potato chips, pretzels, a few bottles of soda, and some party hats, and I invited my aunts and uncles, Dora next door with a couple of her sons, and Millie Adams. Absurd, really—or just wishful thinking on my part. Of course, Gi was nowhere to be found.

It was a surprise party, and no one was more surprised than my mother. I don't know why I did it, and I shudder when I remember all the shell-shocked voices singing, "...happy anniversary, dear Frances and Gi...happy anniversary to you." It was probably an attempt to will my father home.

Sometimes, not often, Blackie sent some money. I had to go stand outside the drug store on 79th Street and wait for him. Blackie would give me a wad of bills (mostly singles) and tell me to put them in my bloomers and run home and give the money to my mother.

Sometimes, I saw Blackie driving a cab in the neighborhood, and he passed me by. Maybe he really didn't see me.

We went on home relief (now called welfare) for about 6 months after Mandrake disappeared. Boxes of powdered milk and institution-size pancake mix. Richard and I had a pancake-eating contest. He ate 16 and won. I never looked at a pancake again.

The welfare worker was very kind. My mother was mortified to be on government assistance, so she got a job at Metropolitan Life Insurance Company with the help of Aunt Phylly. She used the same story that the high school burned down. She became a comptometer operator. It was a big cash register kind of machine (you can see it in the film *The Apartment*). Her take-home pay was 27 dollars a week. I had to watch Joseph, do the laundry and ironing, and start supper. In those days, my mother's beautiful dimples began to look more and more like life-worn lines.

Sometimes, Blackie would call us (when we had a phone), and Frances asked for some money. I don't know what he said on the other end.

I just remember my mother saying, "How am I supposed to raise these kids?"

Joseph was always, always, in the background, yelling. "Ask Daddy when he's coming home!"

Bad times.

This went on, as I wrote, until Blackie eventually came home, welcomed by his loving wife and son, Joseph. Richard was already married (to escape, I think) and had no feelings for his father at that time.

I resented his coming back. It took several months of, "You're not my father. Don't tell me what to do," until he sat me down at the table and said, "I'm asking for a chance. You'd give a dog another chance, wouldn't you?"

That was the beginning of a 20-year wonderful life.

CHAPTER TEN
PRAYERS, DREAMS, AND NIGHTMARES

Now I lay me down to sleep, I pray the Lord my soul to keep. If I should die before I wake, I pray the Lord my soul to take.

There's nothing like speaking about death before tucking a child in for the night, to make her feel secure. My mother never knew that the reason I asked her to tuck the blankets so tight was that I didn't want the Lord to take my soul without a struggle. Frances also never knew that the reason I'd ask her for a million things before letting her leave my side was that I always hoped she would kiss me goodnight. Just once. She was always kind and obliging, and a real good tucker, but never a hug or a kiss. It wasn't her style.

After Frances turned out the light and I was alone in my bed, I prayed in earnest, every night, for years, the prayer that sustained me. This is not a joke. Roy Rogers and Dale Evans were my real parents, and, somehow, there was a mix-up and I ended up in the wrong place.

I knew that someday, everyone would discover the mistake, and I would be restored to the Double R Bar Ranch where I really belonged. Roy, my real father, would take me for rides on Trigger, and I could sleep in the barn with Buttercup, if I wanted. There'd be Bullet to play with, and I would feed chickens, collect eggs, milk cows, and roll around in grass and mud.

It would be wonderful to live under an open sky, far away from the soot of the El. My mother, Dale, would help me pick out wonderful fringed cowgirl outfits, hats with strings, and spangled boots—beautiful clothes I'd get to wear on our television show. It was only a matter of time...I'd be on the ranch with Roy and Dale. It wasn't that I didn't love my parents, it's just that I was sure they weren't mine. *"Happy trails to you, until we meet again..."*

In sleep, my dreams were sometimes not so promising. I was never sure why I dreamed the most horrific dreams. Maybe it was because of *The Early Show*. Or, too many *Million Dollar Movie* nights? These movies were shown nightly on television, after dinnertime. *Million Dollar Movie's* theme song came from the *Gone With The Wind* score, and *The Early Show* featured "The Syncopated Clock," also used for *The Late Show*. I remember that *Million Dollar Movie* showed the same movie all week. By Wednesday, we all lip-synced the dialogue.

Two nightmares plagued me until I was in my teens. The first involved Japanese soldiers jumping from a moving train to the ledge of my window and climbing into my room. For some reason, they never saw me but moved to the other rooms, where they stabbed my family to death with bayonets.

The other dream took me into a wooded area, where, in a cave, lived a witch that made Margaret Hamilton look like Mother Goose. The dream never varied. I'd crouch behind a bush while watching my family walk out of her cave like zombies, all of them dead, but walking, with knives sticking out of their eyes, chanting, "She deathens before me, she deathens before me." Calling Dr. Freud!

There were good dreams, too. I dreamed once that God allowed me to spend one day with a person who had already died. I chose the Marx Brothers. It was a glorious dream. For 24 hours, I was able to join in the antics of my favorite comics at their most outrageous. The dream ended in a supermarket when a great, white light descended in the produce department, and the Marx Brothers instantly stopped tossing tomatoes and announced that they had to leave. It didn't make me sad to see them merge into the light. It was enough for me to remember that I actually spent a day with the Marx Brothers.

My dreams unleashed a much more creative self in me. In one of my dreams, I wrote a play called *You Look Familiar*. It was about identical twins separated at birth who grew up right next door to each other but never met. I have no idea how the play unfolded. I only remember the end, when the twins finally meet, look at each other, and declare in unison, "You look familiar!" The play was a smash on Broadway, and I was up for a Tony.

It was easy to dream when you lived under the El. I suppose dreams of the Japanese and of a wicked witch were to remind me that it could have been worse, but the sweet dreams whispered a promise that much more was possible.

THE BIG GREEN LEATHER CHAIR

I'm not sure this belongs in this chapter. Perhaps it should be part of El Amenities. Not even sure it was leather. It could have been Naugahyde. I know it wasn't a dream—more a nightmare and a prayer. It is something, however, that I will never forget.

It's incredible to think that a chair, an ordinary

chair, would have its own place in this chronicle and in my memory. I can remember every stick of furniture at 8018 New Utrecht Avenue, but all of it was generic. Benign. But not the big green leather chair. That's what it was called...the big green leather chair, as if it was knighted by a king. Everyone agreed that it was regal looking, and even better, so very comfortable. But, it did not belong.

To begin with, the chair was too large for the tiny cold water flat. It looked ridiculous, as if it could suck all the oxygen out of the room. Frances moved it all over the apartment. Its first stop was against the wall between the bathroom and the kitchen. Problem was that the table and chairs needed to be moved, leaving the light fixture dangling above nothing and everyone having to duck to avoid crashing into it, or getting strangled by the hanging cord.

Next stop was a short stay in the corner by one of the windows. But, each time we had to hang clothes on the line, the big green obstacle had to be dragged away to leave room to reach the window.

It finally made its way to the middle of the middle room, at the edge of the high-riser, against the curtain that separated the middle room from my parents' cove. A good spot for anyone who wanted to watch television in a kind of luxury.

For me, the big green leather chair brings back one of the worst memories of my life, right up there with Blackie leaving and Richard moving to Death Valley in the Southwest. To this day, I don't know what a 4 or 5-year-old could have done to warrant the punishment of the threat of banishment to a home for bad children.

I can remember my mother smoking away, silent, sitting in the chair with the ashtray on its wide arm. This was after she got off the phone with the "people from the home," telling them that she would have me ready to leave when they came for me. It was a cruel ruse. All I knew was that I was going to be sent away, never to return.

This memory—my sobs, begging Frances in between gulps of air, promising to never again do whatever it was I'd done, a little girl on my knees looking so small next to that humongous chair with my mother staring straight ahead, ignoring me until I fell in a faint on the floor—is as clear today as it was almost 70 years ago.

When she thought I'd had enough, she went to the phone, dialed a number, and spoke into the phone. "I'm giving her another chance, so you don't have to come for her this time."

I will say again...what the hell could a little girl have done to give her mother no choice but to send her away? Kids are not logical. A sense of security trumps comfort. Maybe the home had a bigger television and a better menu. All I know is that I wanted to stay home and take a lukewarm bath once a week, and freeze in the winter and roast in the summer. I wanted to stub my toe on the *abranda*. I wanted to stay home.

This is difficult to write, but it is part of my memories of life under the El. I remember my mother as always being there for us, putting food on the table, looking at our homework, chasing us down at suppertime, asking neighbors to keep an eye on us if we played *around the corner*, threatening anyone who tried to harm us, playing the piano, and laughing at anything my father said. This is the Frances I will remember, cherish...and I will try to understand that her life was very difficult, and maybe, just maybe, she didn't realize the harm in her actions while sitting in the big green leather chair.

EPILOGUE
ESCAPE FROM STEEL AND SOOT

It wasn't easy for me to leave the cold water flat, with its water bugs, no hot water, icy linoleum floors, stinky hallway, soot-covered walls, roaring El train, and the steel that held it up and housed our special birds of darkness...bugged-eyed bats. Funny how we cling to what's familiar, even if it's unpleasant.

It was the home I knew from birth to 16. I carved my initials in the downstairs front door, and they are still there. As if the memories were not ingrained enough in my brain, there's physical proof that I lived there. I cried the day we left. I kissed the dark red molding goodbye.

I couldn't sleep at first. I missed the "Lullaby in Screech" and the mixed aroma of gas, soot, boiling cabbage, Old Spice, Chanel No. 5, lye soap, Vitalis Hair Tonic, and my mother's comforting lentils and potatoes. Those odors were stuck to the walls.

The first move, in 1965, was up the block to a 4-story walk-up apartment building on 18th Avenue and 81st Street. We were on the top floor. We could still hear the train, but we were now one of the "in the shadow of the El" people on whose lives the El had little effect.

The floors were still linoleum. But, we had some bonuses—sunlight streaming through a couple of windows, a slightly better-smelling hallway, and, best of all, hot running water—any time of the day and night! It was 3 flights up, though, and carrying groceries was no picnic. When my mother or I went food shopping, we used the *carrozza* (carriage), a 2-wheeled metal basket. Thumping it up the stairs made it easier to carry the bags (all paper in those days).

The game of musical beds began in earnest in this one-bedroom apartment. One bed, one sofa bed, and the ever-popular floor. We managed. Well, we all slept, at least. It got somewhat easier when Richard escaped via a too-young marriage, and, for the most part, I slept with Frances, while Joseph got the sofa bed. This created its own déjà vu, because when the bed was open and someone went to use the bathroom, invariably, a toe was stubbed on the bed's metal leg.

Life went on for all of us. Blackie came home to stay when the first grandchild arrived, my niece, Francine. The freelance father and the steely-spined mother joined forces in a mutual love that cannot be described here. It was miraculous. All the years before fell away, and there was new life in the family—a baby girl. A common object of adoration.

God, it was wonderful while it lasted. Blackie was home to stay. Of course, a leopard doesn't change his spots, but for Frances, it didn't matter. The leopard didn't stray too far or too often. But, other forces emerged, and life took another turn, leaving sadness in its wake.

Nonetheless, I am grateful for those days with Francine, and then Richard II—beautiful babies to love and spoil. We also had Joseph's gorgeous daughter, Catherine, right next door until she was 3 years old, when her mother took her to California. That was a heartbreak.

One of the last things my mother said to me was, "I'll never see my Cathy again."

She was right.

After a year of schlepping everything up 3 flights, we moved to 19th Avenue and 81st Street to another apartment building, which was named Foremost Apartments. In its heyday, I'm sure it was very foremost. It made no difference to us, as its luxury days were long gone. We still had a one-bedroom, but we had a reprieve from the stair gods and only walked up 2 flights.

I remember Spumoni Gardens restaurant, still thriving today, and the lots all the way to Cropsey Avenue before the huge apartment buildings took over, and the charlotte russe desserts in their freestanding refrigerators outside the toy store (Zeskins?) on 86th Street. Eighty-sixth Street itself, from 18th Avenue to 25th Avenue with all the stores. Roll-a-Rama. Jahn's. The Loew's Oriental Theatre and its majestic stairs. Enticing aromas from Bauer's Bakery. The candy store on New Utrecht and 81st Street. Gardenia's Deli. Kids on bikes. Kids outside. Mothers in dresses. Feasts in honor of Catholic saints with the chosen saint parading down the street wearing money pinned to its religious garb, and the sausage and peppers at those feasts (for a quarter!)...and much more.

They're alive in my mind now. They'll go when my mind goes.

Everyone scattered. Joseph was drafted, and after his service, he moved around the country for a time but made it back to Bensonhurst, or, as I call it, "The Womb." Richard moved to the Southwest to count cacti and trip over tumbleweeds, and he had more beautiful babies. I got married. Frances and Blackie moved into Aunt Tillie's building—the 2-bedroom, where, in due course, they both died.

Some of the kids from *around the corner* inherited their parents' homes, sold the houses, and moved to Staten Island or New Jersey. Some stayed in the womb of Bensonhurst, Bath Beach, or Dyker Heights. The neighborhoods are all different now.

The babies in our family keep coming. More than 2 dozen, as of this writing. All wonderful. None from me, though. I have cats and dogs. Cheaper.

It is for these beautiful and wonderful nieces and nephews—some of whom now have babies and grandbabies of their own with names my grandparents would have wondered about—that I penned this book of memories.

I hope it will be received well by my family, with the love with which it was written.

The 3 little bastards

Aunt Mary, Uncle John, and baby Theresa

Cousin Ronnie and
Cousin Bobby

Aunt Millie

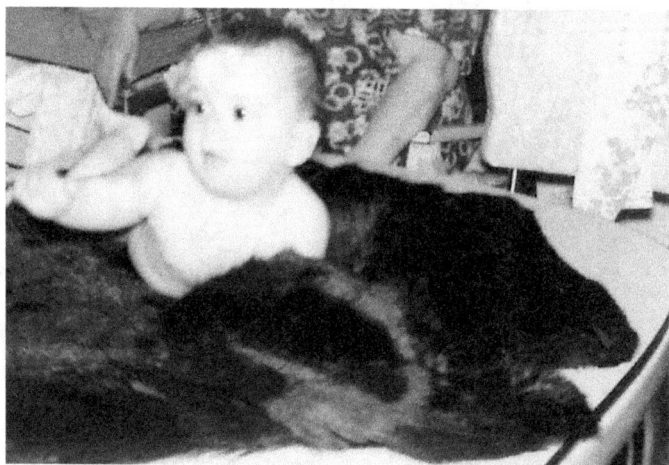
Joseph on Aunt Louise's "alpaca" coat

Cousin Tony and Cousin Bobby

Aunt Louise and Great Aunt Elvira

Uncle Rico

Blackie (Gi) with Skippy

Grandpa Antonio, Grandma Emelia, Gi,
Uncle John, and Uncle Tony Trivone

Grandma Francesca

Richard and Joanne
at Easter time

Aunt Louise and
Aunt Mary

Frances, Joseph, and Joanne—her first Communion

Aunt Mary, Theresa, Anthony, and Joanne

Frances at window under the El—"Come and eat!"

Grandma Francesca

Richard and Joanne on an overworked horse

Frances, Theresa, and Aunt Phylly

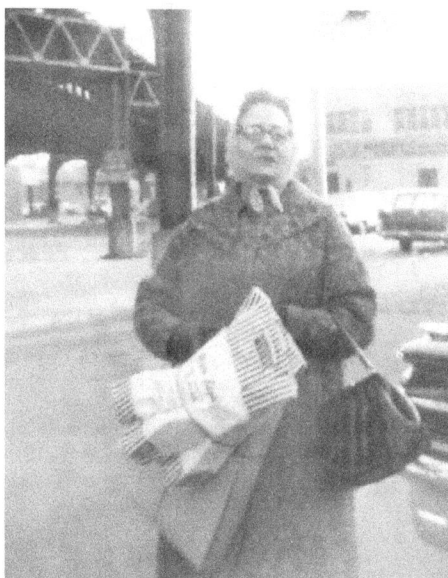

Aunt Phylly—where the El meets *around the corner*

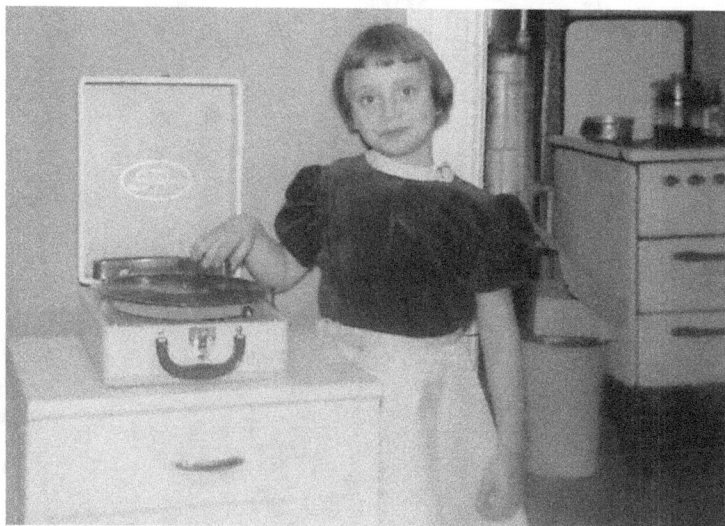

Joanne on her 7th birthday with her new record player

Joanne and Jackie

Richard and Joanne

Joseph on another poor horse

Joanne, Cousin Bobby, and Richard

Some family and friends

Frances and Joanne on her 5th birthday

Joanne on the day
Aunt Louise and Bobby left

Frances and her god-
child, Annette (Bugie)

Joanne — *around the corner*

ABOUT THE AUTHOR

Joanne de Simone is an author, dramatist, poet, and film historian. She was host of "Notes & Notions from The Writing Desk" at LTV-East Hampton Public Access Television, and a weekly guest on Haim Mizrahi's "Hello Hello."

Joanne has written 12 plays, including "Suicide Angel," which is in feature film pre-production. Joanne's film, "White Caps," produced by the Viking Theater Company, was presented at NewFilmmakers in NYC. Her film review column was published in the "Fire Island News" from 1998-2003. Joanne's books include, "The Metro Cats: Life in the Core of the Big Apple," a children's book, "The Peculiar Plight of Milicent Wryght," a young adult urban tale—both set in Manhattan—and "Mating Habits Couples Guide a-z." She also penned, "Lovers. Husbands. Strangers," a baby boomer's chronicle of lust, love, and one-night stands under her pen name, L. L. Ferris.

Ms. de Simone is a member of the Dramatists Guild of America, Shakespeare Guild, and the Academy of American Poets. She holds a BA in Film, Literature, and Creative Writing and lives on the east end of Long Island, New York.

www.ingramcontent.com/pod-product-compliance
Lightning Source LLC
La Vergne TN
LVHW051631080426
835511LV00016B/2299